EX LIBRIS

UNIVERSITATIS SANCTI JOANNIS

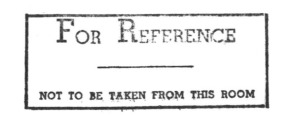

ESSAYS IN MUSICAL ANALYSIS
CHAMBER MUSIC

ESSAYS IN MUSICAL ANALYSIS

By

DONALD FRANCIS TOVEY

CONTENTS

I. SYMPHONIES

II. SYMPHONIES (II), VARIATIONS, AND
ORCHESTRAL POLYPHONY

III. CONCERTOS

IV. ILLUSTRATIVE MUSIC

V. VOCAL MUSIC

VI. SUPPLEMENTARY ESSAYS, GLOSSARY, AND INDEX

SUPPLEMENTARY VOLUME. CHAMBER MUSIC

ESSAYS IN
MUSICAL ANALYSIS
CHAMBER MUSIC

By

DONALD FRANCIS TOVEY

Sometime Reid Professor of Music in the
University of Edinburgh

With an Editor's Note by
HUBERT J. FOSS

LONDON
OXFORD UNIVERSITY PRESS
NEW YORK   TORONTO

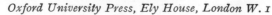
Oxford University Press, Ely House, London W. 1

GLASGOW NEW YORK TORONTO MELBOURNE WELLINGTON
CAPE TOWN SALISBURY IBADAN NAIROBI LUSAKA ADDIS ABABA
BOMBAY CALCUTTA MADRAS KARACHI LAHORE DACCA
KUALA LUMPUR HONG KONG TOKYO

First Published 1944
Sixth Impression 1967

PRINTED IN GREAT BRITAIN

EDITOR'S NOTE

AT times, the late Sir Donald Tovey spoke to me about his analyses of chamber music, including those of works written for piano solo. I was born a little too late fully to have understood the significance of his references. Now that I have seen and read the programmes of the remarkable concerts which Tovey organized and played at in the St. James's Hall in London in 1900 and 1901, I feel back and find myself in close sympathy with that astonishing young man of 25 who gave to the world a collection of masterpieces of music, with lucid expositions of them in his notes, and under their shadow caught the sunlight with his own compositions.

The notes that come from the turn of the century are brilliant, detailed, and extensive. There is a particular flavour about them, with the scent of those concerts still clinging, that is unequalled even in the Reid Orchestra's notes, now known as *Essays in Musical Analysis*. They do not attempt to cover the range of classical chamber music, which is discussed in general in the first essay. Tovey, as we know, seldom theorized about music in general unless he had a necessity to write about a piece in particular, which he was about to perform at once or in the near future. The gaps, alas, cannot be filled; nevertheless, we have here the varied wealth of Tovey's musical thought, while he writes about Chopin or Brahms or Bach in the most precise terms.

To the items in the list of contents at the beginning of the volume, I have added the dates of the author's writing. They range from 1900 to 1936, and no attempt has been made to adapt the style of one period or purpose to that of another, or to make a homogeneous whole of the book. It was in the author's mind to do some work of adaptation himself: thus he wrote in 1935 of the 'Goldberg' essay, 'Possibly I may get it digested into something equally complete and more terse'. But this task he did not fulfil. Some repetitions have been removed—notably the short remarks (of 1936) on the 'Goldberg' Variations, which would appear perfunctory alongside the magnificent complete analysis (of 1900).

While the St. James's Hall concerts are beyond my memory, the gramophone recording of *Die Kunst der Fuge*, for which the essay of that work herein included was written, is not. For, with no clear aim, I thought it wise to pay a visit to the recording studio on the morning when Tovey was playing on the piano his own completion of the final fugue, and was instantly conscribed by Tovey to play the returning main subject in the bass.

I have the permission of Lady Tovey to collect and reprint these chamber music analyses in a volume, and for this and for her help in all ways I warmly acknowledge my indebtedness to her and offer my thanks. I have also to record my thanks to Messrs. Joseph Williams, Ltd., the first enterprising publishers of the early notes, by whose permission they are printed here; to the British Broadcasting Corporation and to the Editor of the *Listener* for leave to reprint the article on *Die Clavierübung* of Bach; to the Columbia Graphophone Company, Ltd., for leave to reprint 'The Listener's Guide to *Die Kunst der Fuge*', issued by that company as a companion pamphlet to the album of records; and to Mr. A. A. Pearson for the essay on Chamber Music from *Cobbett's Cyclopedic Survey of Chamber Music*. To Dr. Mary Grierson, Dr. Ernest Walker, and Mr. R. C. Trevelyan I owe the warmest gratitude, both for help and advice, and because by reading the proofs they have kept me in a narrow path of comparative accuracy, which alone I could hardly have followed.

HUBERT J. FOSS

1943

CONTENTS

vii

BRAHMS

CHAMBER MUSIC

I. A GENERAL SURVEY
(1928)

LIKE most classical terms, chamber music has meant different things at different periods, and has developed by evolution. It is a mistake to try to reduce early and late products of an evolutionary process to a common definition. There are theoretical objections to any limit that can be proposed. These may be removed by a statement which clearly shows the relation of what is excluded from the main scope of this essay to what is included.

The great change which came over the whole art of music after the middle of the eighteenth century affected chamber music no less profoundly than it affected opera. Nobody would quarrel with a history of opera for beginning with Gluck, so long as it did not wholly ignore his antecedents, archaic, prophetic, and decadent. But the kind of operatic art from which Gluck revolted rested on principles so radically and, to our notions, so obviously wrong, that all attempts to revive it must savour of antiquarianism. This is not the case with the chamber music of the earlier eighteenth century; its principles, though now obsolete, were consistent and true to the nature of the instruments, and its masterpieces can never become antiquated. And their quantity is enormous. The whole mass of the chamber music of Bach, Handel, the Italian violin masters, and the French clavecinists must be far more voluminous than the sum-total of important chamber music from Haydn onwards, even if vocal music be excluded. And to review it, or even to read a review of it, is a task at which librarians might quail.

Fortunately for the reader, though it cannot be ruled out on artistic grounds, it is all based on two principles which are radically opposed to those of the later classical chamber music. Accordingly, my first part is devoted to illustrating the theory and practice of the continuo in the earlier chamber music, with occasional remarks on the other archaic principle, the mechanical use of 4-foot and 16-foot stops on the harpsichord and organ, the instruments to which the continuo was entrusted.

Though much has been written about the continuo, no writer has hitherto shown its relation to the aesthetics of later chamber music. But unless this relation is clearly understood, we cannot properly understand the revolution effected by Haydn and Mozart, nor fully appreciate the qualities of purity and euphony in chamber-music style. The continuo and the use of 4-foot and

16-foot doublings represent important musical instincts. To ignore or misunderstand them is to deprive the earlier chamber music of its euphony.

In the later chamber music the continuo instinct sometimes reasserts itself (often without the composer's realizing its origin) as an impurity of style; especially when he is in the habit of composing at the piano.

THE CONTINUO PERIOD

For general purposes, chamber music may be defined as instrumental music written for a group of individual performers, and intended to be heard for its own sake in such rooms as are to be found in private houses. Dance music, and music intended 'to accompany the clatter of dishes at a princely table', exclude themselves from the category of music intended to be heard for its own sake.

The size of the room is not a matter for rigid definition; the hundred-and-fifty years during which the classics of chamber music were composed were a period of royal and aristocratic patronage, and the rooms for which the music was designed were the rooms of palaces. And it is not an unmixed evil that chamber music should be heard in halls that are too large for it. The necessity can arise only because of a remarkable public demand for the highest and most spiritual form of music, and the acoustic disadvantages have a distinct value as a stimulus to the imagination. The listener naïve enough to expect the ff of Schubert's D minor Quartet to sound loud in a concert-room holding an audience of 2,000, learns in five minutes to prefer spiritual to material values in music, if he can learn anything.

Nevertheless, the classical idea of chamber music implies bigness as well as intimacy, and the listener is not enjoying the normal effect of a trio or quartet unless the sound is filling the room. This classical notion of bigness determines the art-forms; no classical chamber music is merely lyric. Beethoven's Fugue in D major, op. 137, for string quintet takes less than four minutes to play, and begins and ends softly; but fugues are not lyrics, and Beethoven's sketches for this opusculum are entangled with ideas of a fugal opening which afterwards took shape in the scherzo of the Ninth Symphony. Other short pieces of chamber music are either large sets of variations or fragments of projected complete sonata-schemes. Schumann's *Märchenerzählungen* and Dvořák's 'Dumky' Trio are exceptional groups of lyrics by composers who otherwise accept the classical view that a chamber work must contain at least one movement in developed sonata form. This rule is a natural result of the feeling that when two or more people are gathered together to play music, they may as well take the opportunity of doing more than can be done by one person. In Germany it is even considered a solecism to call a duet concert a chamber concert; chamber music is held to begin with trios. An upper limit has not been assigned. Mozart's Serenade in B flat for thirteen wind instruments is, for reasons which will appear in the course of this essay, within the limits of classical chamber music, though even the most experienced wind players will feel in its performance that a conductor adds much to the comfort of a group that is twice the size of the wind band of any symphony before Beethoven.

Mozart's group of thirteen, however, does not include trumpets and drums, that is to say, it includes nothing which is either enormously stronger in tone than the rest of the ensemble or enormously inferior to it in musical resource. The trumpet in Saint-Saëns's little Septet is almost the only instance of the introduction of such powerful orchestral artillery into chamber music in a classical style, and here the classical style is jocosely archaic.

The double-bass (or, as in Mozart's Serenade, the contra-bassoon) does undoubtedly bring into chamber music the question of inferiority in musical resource. This will be discussed later, but here we may conveniently note that inferiority in musical resource is not to be measured by the amount of conspicuous display, whether in melody or flourishes, but by the necessity for the use of the instrument. And the double-bass may obviously be very necessary for the support of so large a group as eight or more instruments.

The criteria thus far indicated for classical chamber music seem simple and not formidably exacting. Every part is to be necessary, and the ensemble is to be complete in itself. Therefore an instrumental group must be capable of making a coherent ensemble, so that, whatever the art employed in combining sounds on different planes of tone, the chamber music style does not encourage the use either of an instrument which cannot be allowed to use its normal strength, or of one which cannot make itself heard without constant strain on its own part and constant repression of the other instruments.

Obvious as this all seems, there is a whole classical period in which none of these criteria can be taken literally. The main life-work of Haydn may be regarded as devoted to organizing the art of making groups of instruments cohere as effectively as groups of voices. Instruments do not normally so cohere, and the commonest form of bad instrumentation is that of the composer whose orchestral and quartet writing is choral and organ music distributed among combinations of instruments. The worst feature of such a style is that it does not sound obviously bad, except to a highly experienced and discriminating ear, which resents the feeling of wasted opportunity as immediately as an insulting cacophony, for the grammar of the chorus and the organ has a universal validity in virtue of which its use as a basis for instrumentation may best be vindicated and condemned by the term 'fool-proof'. But during the period of supreme mastery of the chorus and the organ which culminated in Bach and Handel, nothing is more significant than the absolute and instinctive renunciation of all attempts to make groups of instruments cohere in the same way as groups of voices. Haydn showed how to make them do so as effectively, but on principles fundamentally different; this he could never have done if the masters before him had not cultivated their sense of the different planes of instrumental sounds with minds untroubled by the problem of focusing the planes together. Nor were they wrong in neglecting this problem. Difference of plane gives rise to an enormous number of the highest aesthetic qualities in all arts; and there is no imperfection in a scheme of instrumental music in which the main parts are left completely free to execute polyphonic designs, while the task of supporting these designs with a coherent mass of harmony is relegated to a continuo player extemporizing on a suitable keyboard instrument from a figured bass.

In modern performances of such music grave errors may arise from ignorance of two matters which were common knowledge to all Bach's musical contemporaries: first, the art of filling out a figured continuo part, and, second, the general characteristics of early eighteenth-century musical forms. Without a careful explanation of these matters it is impossible to appreciate the immensity of the task achieved by Haydn and Mozart, an immensity hardly understood by any of their contemporaries, in obtaining the harmonic background from the principal instruments themselves without the aid of any permanently subordinate part. Until this was achieved, chamber music could not be defined as an ensemble to which each player contributes an individual part. For not only did the individual parts themselves not claim to be complete without the impersonal continuo, but the very notion of an individual part was purely musical, and independent of the number of performers. Bach's organ trios are trios for two manuals and a pedal-board, to be played by one organist. But his trio in *Das Musikalische Opfer*, for flute, violin, and continuo, realizes its intended effect only when four instruments play it, viz. the flute, the violin, a 'cello to play the bass of the continuo, and a keyboard instrument to fill out the harmonies according to the figures. Without the 'cello to lift the bass of the continuo on to its proper plane as one of the three trio parts, the mere filling out on the keyed instruments fails to complete a trio in Bach's sense.

In modern times four great errors arise in the treatment of the continuo. First, there is the total omission to fill it out—an error which so little impairs Bach's gorgeous polyphony that most listeners devoutly admire the resulting coldness of tone as a mysterious classical virtue. Secondly, there is the filling-out with a tone on the same plane as the real parts—an error impossible to a harpsichord player, who had but to draw the right stops for an accompaniment instead of playing on solo or tutti registers. The third error is the attempt to work out the figuring in a kind of polyphony that competes with the real parts. The fourth and worst error is the filling out with parts that avoid doubling or otherwise colliding with the main lines. This error is assiduously inculcated by theorists who also fiercely denounce the substitution of the piano for the harpsichord. But the piano is, as Philipp Emanuel Bach pointed out, even better than the harpsichord for continuo work, only it must be remembered that the contemporaries of Bach's sons knew both instruments, and could make no mistakes as to the kind of piano touch required. A piano filling-out can be made into an ideally soft background, but the instincts of the average modern pianist do not incline that way, and nothing can be more banal than the intrusion of an ordinary pianistic mezzo-forte into the background tone of an eighteenth-century polyphonic design. The error of a too elaborate polyphony in continuo work rests upon records of Bach's own marvellous freedom therein, but a little practical experience shows that ordinary skill in handling harmonic progressions will, with the aid of an occasional imitation of four notes of a scale in thirds or in contrary motion, cause the naïve listener to gasp with astonishment, and spread abroad the legend that everything has been decorated in six-part canonic counterpoint. As a fact in practice and aesthetics, nothing is more miserable than the attempt to fill out Bach's polyphony with additional individual counterpoints. The efforts of Robert Franz were thought, in their own day in the middle of the nineteenth century, to be indistinguishable from Bach's own real parts. At the present day it is hard to understand how anybody could have thought such bundles of dropped stitches and loose ends acceptable on any theory, though worse things have been perpetrated in more recent editions of Bach.

The fourth error is all the worse for the erudition that is still spent on its cultivation. Franz, in his edition (Breitkopf and Härtel's *Kammermusik-Bibliothek*) of Bach's trio (from *Das Musikalische Opfer*), condemns the continuo realization by Bach's masterly pupil Kirnberger as a setting that 'tramples on all the fine flower of Bach's polyphony'. Unfortunately it is Franz's own setting that tramples on the fine flower, systematically, and exactly as he differs from Kirnberger. Franz thinks of the filling-out as on the same plane of tone as the main parts, or, to conceive the matter conversely, he thinks of the ensemble as it would sound if the flute and violin were played on one piano and the continuo on another. In such conditions a collision between a plain chord and the same chord plus a long appoggiatura would be hideous, as any one may satisfy himself by playing the D major cantabile theme in Beethoven's G major Concerto on two pianos instead of one piano with orchestra. But when the sounds are on different planes, the chords on the lower plane must always be complete in themselves, and should seldom double even the weightier ornamental discords of the main parts. No harshness whatever can result from collisions between ornamental notes in the main planes and essential chords in the background, nor between two distinct main planes. Bach, in this very sonata, rejoices in collisions between the violin and the flute which he would not have allowed between two violins. Kirnberger's continuo is right in two important matters: first, that it gives Bach's essential chords completely without doubling his ornamental discords, and second, that it is in strict four-part harmony. But it gives no countenance to the impossible theory that such four-part writing must avoid moving in unison with the main parts. Such asceticism can never have been attempted in real life, for the continuo-player never had anything but his figured bass to play from, and so could not have dodged unisons with the main part however much he might wish to do so. And to succeed therein is only to violate one of the first principles of instrumentation, viz. that when two or more bodies of sound are on different planes, each must be intelligible by itself whatever the others may add to its meaning. The idea that the continuo-filling could ever have attempted to avoid doubling the main parts cannot survive one intelligent perusal of the relation between voices and orchestra in any chorus of Bach or Handel where the orchestra has florid independent parts.

But though Kirnberger is true to his art and technique in setting his continuo in four real parts, the intention of his setting is not adequately represented merely by playing it softly on the modern piano. Bach's harpsichord had 16-foot as well as 4-foot stops, and we know from his first biographer Forkel that he was so impatient of gaps in the middle of the continuo harmony that he would often put in 'three new parts' (i.e. a handful of inner notes) over the continuo-player's shoulder. It so happens that the only practical normal position for continuo harmonies is for the right hand to play three notes to a chord at a safe distance from the bass. The drift of the suspensions and other discords is sure to go downwards, and the bass is sure to rise frequently, until the harmony is forced into close quarters and will have to spring apart again. But the 16-foot register of the harpsichord, or the lieblich gedackt stop of the choir organ, fills up the gap exquisitely softly, and the piano can reproduce the effect either by filling out the chords extremely fully, or by taking almost everything an octave lower, in either case with the smoothest pianissimo and no sense of percussion at all. A 'cello should always be used to play the bass throughout in as cantabile a style as the upper instruments, and the pianist should refrain from doubling its ornaments and rapid details.

The following example from the beginning of the trio in *Das Musikalische Opfer* will show the principles involved. Here (Ex. 1) is the ensemble of flute, violin, and continuo, the main part of this last being played by a 'cello. (Note the collision Bach allows between violin and flute in bar 6.) And here (Ex. 2) is a schematic filling-out of the figuring on Kirnberger's lines, but with the assumption that a 'cellist is playing from his own part so that its throbbing rhythm and expressive details (e.g. the theme in bar 5) need not be doubled by the modern piano.

And this is the sort of way in which the piano can compensate for the loss of the 16-foot register of Bach's harpsichord; the quaver rest in the fifth bar being designed to let light upon the 'cello with its theme (Ex. 3).

Ex. 3

Kirnberger, whose copy of the continuo evidently differed from the original score in detail, as all Bach's various copies differ from each other, often takes account of the long appoggiaturas in bars 1 and 3, which are neglected on principle here. Sometimes such points are in the figuring. But it would be a fundamental error to fill out the first bar thus—

Ex. 4

taking its final anticipation as seriously as the complete triad at the end of bar 5. And the attempt to avoid unisons between the continuo and the main parts could only lead to such miseries as

Ex. 5

which no human touch could render a tolerable filling-up of Bach's harmony.

From all this it is clear that it was a mighty task to bridge the gulf between chamber music on the continuo hypothesis and the dramatic sonata style of Haydn and Mozart, with its substitution of pure instrumental self-sufficiency for depersonalized melodic polyphony. Perhaps the most important fact which separates the earlier from the later chamber music is the power of harpsichord registers to multiply the written sounds in different octaves. This power, which the organ develops on an incomparably larger scale, utterly obliterates the qualities on which chamber music from Haydn onwards is based, and it is this, rather than the accident of ecclesiastical associations, that has debarred even a small domestic organ or (*pace* Dvořák) the best of harmoniums from sharing in anything that we now call chamber music.

' The art forms of early instrumental music are embodied with such crystalline clearness and solidity by Bach, and the conceptions underlying them are so essential to a correct understanding of how to perform not only his works, but those of Purcell and Handel, that a mention of the main elements is essential. The dance forms used in Corelli's sonata da camera are obviously in line with those of the suite, partita, or ordre. Corelli's type of sonata da chiesa, with its introductory or intermediary adagios and its fugal allegros, is an equally obvious origin of Lully's French overture; and the French overture, again, stimulated by the importance of the ballet in French opera from the earliest times, after beginning like a sonata da chiesa, naturally develops the forms of the sonata da camera in a series of dance tunes.

Another early art form to which Purcell and Biber clung as if to save themselves from drowning in the pathless ocean of early instrumental music was the ground-bass, a form which by its constant repetition of a single sentence in the bass provided a rigid principle, immediately intelligible and capable of indefinite extension and fine cumulative effect. Bach's examples of it in its rigorous form are so famous that we forget that they are very few. In chamber music he developed a modified form in which the ground-bass now and then turns into a new key, so that in about four groups of variations the movement has accomplished a circle of keys without either abandoning or interrupting its ground-bass. The typical example of such a modulating ground is the third movement of Bach's E major Sonata for cembalo and violin.

But the paramount art-form of early eighteenth-century chamber music is derived from the concerto. The origins of concerto form are vocal, and so slight are the barriers between vocal and instrumental art-forms in the early eighteenth century, that Bach, the most accurate exemplar of all forms, is the master who achieved the most astonishing translations from one medium to the other, transcribing concerto movements and overtures into great choruses, and, conversely, turning arias into slow movements of concertos. This explains and almost justifies the policy of the Bach-Gesellschaft editors in classifying all his secular vocal works as chamber music.

Indeed, the continuo period might just as well be called the aria period, and the whole of its chamber music be regarded as primarily vocal; the only objection would be that no definite notion of chamber music would be left. For it makes no great aesthetic difference whether two or three arias are grouped, with

interspersed recitatives, into a chamber cantata, or thirty arias
into an opera, and presented amid gorgeous stage trappings to a
large public. At least three-quarters of Handel's numerous vocal
cantatas are to be found dispersed in his forty-two operas, and it
is a matter of indifference whether the operatic or domestic
environment came first. The essential point is that the principal
art-form of the period was neither the fugue nor the binary dance
form, but the aria. And the form of the aria is precisely that of
the concerto. It depends on the fact that the voice inevitably
thrusts all instrumental sounds into the background. Hence the
most effective way to expand a vocal melody into a big movement
is to let instruments play the gist of it in a single musical para-
graph, so that it becomes lifted to a higher plane when the voice
takes it up and expands it with other themes and brilliant passages. The instrumental ritornello will then intervene, entire or
in part, wherever closes are made in foreign keys, and it will
complete the whole by its final delivery in the tonic.

Now with proper treatment a solo instrument throws an
orchestral tutti into the background as naturally (though not so
forcibly) as the human voice throws all instruments. Hence the
aria form became the foundation of the concerto style as soon
as composers began to value the contrast between solos and
orchestral groups. And this contrast was closely imitated by the
various registers of the organ and the harpsichord, the composite
tones of the octave registers giving a clear representation of tutti
ritornellos, while a solo stop on one manual and a soft accompaniment on the other cannot fail to produce the effect of the entry
of a solo instrument. When we have learnt to recognize this
concerto form wherever it occurs in early chamber music, our
notions of interpretation will be delivered from many an arbitrary
and misleading tradition, and our imagination will have a better
stimulus than guess-work. Of course Bach's Italian Concerto,
for harpsichord alone, is as nearly schematic in its illustration of
the method as a work of genius can be, but it does not stand
alone. In his chamber music almost any large allegro not in
binary form will become clear as soon as we mark out three types
of passage, viz. the tuttis, the solos, and the ensemble passages
which imitate the blending of solo work with independent orchestral detail. Each type of passage should be kept on its own plane
of tone, and, while no artificial restraint should be imposed on
the capacity of modern instruments for expressive nuances, the
players should regard it as nonsensical to drift from one plane of
tone to another in such a way as to blur the lines of concerto
form. No such mistake was possible to the players of Bach's age;
and the composer seldom gave explicit directions, for he could
not foresee that doubt would ever arise.

Every peculiarity of the piano is in keeping with the new and dramatic spirit which entered into all kinds of music from the operas of Gluck to the symphonies and string quartets of Haydn. To those who have in modern times been thrilled by the rediscovery of the organ-like richness of plain two-part writing on a harpsichord with 4-foot and 16-foot registers in play, nothing in the history of the sonata style is more surprising than the cheerfulness with which Mozart and Haydn accepted the renunciation of all attempts to apply such registers to the piano. Henceforth no written note was to represent more sounds than that of its own name and octave. The enrichment of harmony by doubling in octaves must be achieved by individual human fingers or players, and not by mechanical couplers. On the other hand, the sustaining of harmony was no longer exclusively the work of individual fingers; a pedal could prevent the dampers from stopping the sound when the fingers left the key, and so an arpeggio of single notes might leave behind a chord vibrating throughout four or five octaves with a rich and slowly evanescent sound transparent to all other instrumental tones. Thus the sonata ideals of chamber music and the style of the piano stimulated each other, and speedily determined the criteria which are valid from the time of Haydn to the present day. These classical criteria may be formulated under two headings, as follows.

I. Chamber music is music in large forms for a group of solo instruments on equivalent planes of tone and of equivalent musical capacity. The planes of tone need not be the same; on the contrary, the value of the piano in chamber music depends largely on its being inevitably on a different plane from all other instruments, but it has no difficulty in refraining from shattering the ensemble like a trumpet or a trombone, and the ear takes pleasure in low notes on a 'cello as a bass to full chords on the piano, the difference of plane being essential to the special effect. The introduction of the singing voice into the scheme, as in Schönberg's Second String Quartet and Sextet, produces a non-equivalent plane of tone, and accordingly goes beyond the classical criteria. A further step, both as to planes of tone and non-equivalence of musical resource, is shown in Schönberg's *Pierrot Lunaire*, where the singer is required to follow a prescribed rise and fall of pitch in a speaking voice, carefully avoiding definite musical notes. In the opposite direction, Cyril Scott and Arthur Bliss use the singing voice without words in an instrumental ensemble.

The question of equivalent musical capacity was frequently raised in classical masterpieces by the use of the double-bass. In a mature style of chamber music this instrument, which with the best of playing, cannot compete effectively with other stringed instruments in cantabile passages, justifies its existence as a support to large groups, especially such as contain wind instruments, as in Beethoven's Septet and Schubert's Octet. Even so, it associates itself naturally with the lighter and looser style of art typified by the serenades and divertimenti of Mozart. Early in the nineteenth century, Onslow, a prolific writer of chamber music, having occasion to use a double-bass as a makeshift for a 'cello, found the effect so satisfactory that he wrote numerous quintets for two violins, viola, 'cello, and double-bass. It is not clear from his notation in what octave he means the double-bass to play. Even in Dvořák's far more highly organized Quintet in G, the double-bass does not seem quite at ease in the drawing-room, and its one shy cantabile remark in the minuet of Goetz's Piano Quintet is a pathetic triumph of unconscious humour.

Stravinsky's introduction of drums, trombones, and similar artillery into chamber music marks another new epoch with new criteria. What these criteria may be, we shall know when a propagandist arises who can convince us that a totally unprepared extemporization by a dozen players will not pass muster with him as a masterpiece of modern music. Stravinsky knows what he is doing; and experimental art is more important than experimental propaganda.

II. Chamber music requires no more than the number of players for whom individual parts are written; and every note written is intended to be heard. We have seen that chamber music before 1760 did not aim at this criterion; it was created with infinite labour by Haydn. The masters who may be taken as realizing it instinctively and imaginatively from first to last are Mozart, Beethoven, and Brahms. All who have attempted to write chamber music approximate to it at their best moments. But we may here profitably glance at some typical cases where music, otherwise beautiful and important, shows a defective sense of this criterion. It is interesting to note, by the way, that the criterion is never more severely maintained than in the most experimental works of the present day. Indeed, the desire to experiment with non-equivalent planes of tone and non-equivalent musical capacities goes naturally with the utmost sensitiveness to the individuality of each instrument. It is rather to the immediate successors of Beethoven that we must turn for examples of the confusion of thought natural to men who feel secure in a classical tradition not of their own making.

Certain tremolo passages in the string quartets of Mendelssohn are often, and not unfairly, quoted as bad examples of orchestral writing in chamber music. But here we must beware of a worse confusion of thought than Mendelssohn's. There is no harm whatever in one kind of good music sounding like another kind, if it has the virtues of both kinds.

If any good orchestral sounds can be realized by a string quartet, so much the better for the quartet. What is wrong with Mendelssohn's tremolos is that they are conceived mechanically on the analogy of orchestral passages, and carried to lengths which only an orchestra could make acceptable. On paper the storm in the development of the first movement of Beethoven's Quartet, op. 74, looks quite as coarse, but it would at the outset be far too thick for orchestral writing, and its wonderful diminuendo is all drawn exactly to scale in a quartet which, as a whole, is one of the most ethereal compositions ever written. The same praise is due to such apparently crude simplicities as the stiff minims with which the violins and 'cello accompany the viola solo in the second variation of the finale. Dante or Milton never surpassed that calm—

They also serve who only stand and wait.

We are on less slippery ground in dealing with the integrity of the parts in classical chamber music. The immaturity of Haydn's piano trios in this respect is discussed, together with traces of piano ideas in one or two of his string quartets, in my article on Haydn in *Cobbett's Cyclopedic Survey of Chamber Music*, due warning being given there against neglecting to view the value of the parts in relation to the degree of polyphony suited to the style. An honest violinist will be compelled to say that the second violin part of a Mendelssohn quartet is more interesting than that of one by Mozart. But this does not make Mendelssohn a better quartet-writer than Mozart. His work is on such a much larger scale that it often droops and fails, like the full-sized machine of an inventor who does not realize that its powers do not increase in the ratio of its bulk to that of the working model. The sympathetic but critical study of Schumann's chamber music will show more clearly where the criterion applies. With a full and sonorous piano style, he has even more than Haydn's curious inability to refrain from putting into the piano part all that the other parts have to say. Indeed, he has altogether lost the power of sorting out his material into its proper planes, and the exquisite first trio of the scherzo of the Piano Quartet is in such a tangle of useless and arbitrary doublings that it is impossible to discover the persons of the dialogue. Mozart, Beethoven, and Brahms would have delighted in making it stand out as a beautiful dialogue between five singing parts, the three strings, and the pianist's right and left hands, with no confusion between these parts and the supporting chords to which each instrument would contribute between its own distinct entries with the themes. It is impossible to argue that there is aesthetic value in Schumann's unclarified scoring of this passage. The Piano Quartet is more highly organized than its delightful and popular brother the Quintet. But the perversity of inattention to the integrity of parts can hardly be more clearly demonstrated than by the fact that, while the string parts of the Quintet are such a primitive mass of harmony that there is no reason why they should not be arranged for quartet, sextet, or string orchestra, the opening of the Piano Quartet shows serious practical reasons why it should have been a quintet!

We must not confuse the criteria of mere part-writing with those of the treatment of an instrument as a whole. There is no reason why a string quartet should not, by means of double stops, produce a passage that effectively imitates an octet. But there is no excuse for making a string quartet play for pages together in such masses of double stops that there is no more evidence of four individual players than in a piano four-hand duet. It is no defence that such writing (as in Grieg's G minor Quartet) is 'effective'; to prolong it is to do a ridiculously easy thing at the expense of all higher possibilities. César Franck's String Quartet is in this way a disappointment to every one who can appreciate the essential, if sometimes harmlessly orchestral, quintuplicity of his great Piano Quintet. The String Quartet is full of excellent organ music, and it imitates the organ very skilfully. But, except for the scherzo, which is full of anybody's brilliance, there is strangely little evidence that it is a quartet at all.

These criteria are unquestionably correct, whatever disputes may arise as to their application. In conclusion, it may be as well to enumerate, and occasionally comment on, some of the principal combinations used in chamber music, beginning with Haydn.

I. *Duets*

(*a*) Two violins: magnificently exploited by Spohr, whom the severe discipline of this problem stimulated to his best work.

(*b*) Violin and viola, represented by two masterpieces of Mozart written to help Michael Haydn to complete the execution of a commission for six. The extra low fifth of the viola greatly eases the pressure on an imagination confined by the violin to a bass no lower than its open G.

(*c*) Two 'cellos: a magnificent medium, very sonorous in spite of its severe restrictions, and very little explored.

(*d*) Piano and violin. The most frequently attempted form of chamber music, and by far the most treacherous. The progress, from the use of the violin as a hardly necessary accompaniment to its perfect partnership in the ensemble, is beautifully shown in the works of Mozart's childhood, from his seventh year to his twelfth. There is a gap between these and his adult sonatas. With occasional lapses, his later sonatas, like Beethoven's, make severe but legitimate demands on the players' and listeners' capacity to focus the two planes of tone into one picture. For this reason duets for

(e) Piano and 'cello are much easier to write when it occurs to a composer to attempt them. There are far fewer 'cello sonatas of all kinds than violin sonatas in existence; but a much larger proportion of the former is good.

(f) Piano and a wind instrument. Here, as with other combinations, the horn and the clarinet have had the best chances, the flute being inconveniently weak for the piano, the oboe being apt to pall when not frequently relieved by other tones, and the bassoon being insufficiently appreciated except as a comedian, though Mozart wrote a sonata for 'cello and bassoon. Technical limitations, even when so severe as those of the natural horn, do not hamper the composer's imagination once it has been stirred, but he is absolutely inhibited by the suspicion of an incompatibility of tone.

II. *Trios*

(a) String trios for violin, viola, and 'cello are a rare *tour de force* not necessarily less valuable than string quartets. Mozart's Divertimento-trio in E flat is a marvel of euphony, and proceeds for pages together without a double stop. Beethoven's string trios are among the very greatest works of his first period.

(b) Trios for two violins and 'cello are mostly the aftermath of the continuo period.

(c) Trios for piano, violin, and 'cello. Of all combinations with piano this is the one that has stimulated composers to the finest results. Haydn's trios, imperfect as they are in point of integrity of parts, are full of his grandest forms and most pregnant ideas. Mozart sets the standard with his inevitable schematic accuracy. The autographs of his trios are written in a way that shows to the eye one of the important normal criteria of the style. He writes the violin above and the 'cello below the piano. And with all their rich subsequent developments of piano style, both Beethoven and Brahms retained the idea of the 'cello as an independent bass below the piano, but, like Mozart, gave it freedom to mount to its highest regions and neglected none of its possibilities.

The ordinary notation which puts the violin and 'cello together above the piano expresses another fact about the combination: viz. that when the piano is combined with two or more instruments, these tend to form a single antiphonal body of tone.

This is equally the case when a wind instrument enters the combination; the three distinct planes of tone separate easily and naturally into two groups, namely the piano and the other two instruments. Some of the combinations represented by important works are:

(*d*) Piano, clarinet, and viola (Mozart);
(*e*) Piano, clarinet, and violoncello (Brahms, Beethoven);
(*f*) Piano, violin, and horn (Brahms).

The piano and two wind instruments have also been successfully combined, the softest combination being with clarinet and horn. Publishers are reluctant to undertake the sale of such works unless alternative arrangements for more usual instruments are provided. When the composer executes these with freedom, the results are extremely instructive, both where they succeed and where they fail in giving an adequate translation of the original.

(*g*) Among curious trio combinations mention should be made of Beethoven's *tour de force* for two oboes and cor anglais, a full-sized four-movement work within the compass of less than three octaves and with no possibility of a chord in more than three parts. His jocular Serenade for flute, violin, and viola has inspired Reger to two essays in this slender combination.

III. *Quartets*

(*a*) In the string quartet for two violins, viola, and 'cello we have the purest and highest revelation of chamber music and perhaps of all music. Its criteria need no further discussion here.

(*b*) The flute and the oboe have each been deliciously combined with strings in short works by Mozart.

(*c*) Quartets for piano and strings are surprisingly rare considering the popularity of the existing classical examples. Mozart's two masterpieces should have belonged to a set of six. They show with the utmost clearness the principle of setting the strings in antiphonal mass against the piano, and are at the same time exquisitely polyphonic. Later publishers tried to atone for former errors by arranging Mozart's Clarinet Quintet, D major String Quintet, and Quintet for piano and wind, as piano quartets. Nothing can be learnt from these.

Apart from three juvenile essays, Beethoven's only piano quartet is an arrangement of his Quintet for piano and wind, op. 16. The piano part is unchanged, but the string parts are full of excellent new detail inserted during the long rests of the wind instruments, these rests being unnecessary for string players.

Mendelssohn's three juvenile quartets are wonderful for a boy of thirteen, and the third, in B minor, has many intrinsic merits.

After this there is nothing important, except the beautiful Schumann Quartet, before the masterpieces of Brahms.

IV. *Quintets*

(*a*) String quintets differ little from quartets. The favourite extra instrument is a second viola, but, apart from the merely decorative works of the 'cellist Boccherini, the combination with a second 'cello is revealed as a majestic art form by Schubert in his great C major Quintet.

(*b*) The clarinet makes a glorious combination with a string quartet, as has been shown by Mozart and Brahms. Mozart also wrote a charming little quintet for the curious combination of one violin, two violas, 'cello, and horn. His most unclassifiable quintet is the Adagio and Rondo for flute, oboe, viola, 'cello, and glass harmonica, evidently a most skilfully planned combination.

(*c*) Quintets for wind instruments present a peculiar problem, especially centred in the group of the five different members, flute, oboe, clarinet, horn, and bassoon. Even under the stimulus of a prize competition, nothing great has been achieved, though an extraordinary amount has been written for this combination. Towards the middle of the nineteenth century that ingenious calculating-machine, Reicha, turned out an incredible number of such quintets. He was too sure of his ground either to fail in securing euphony or to show why he took all this trouble. The great composers have not been attracted by the problem of making coherent chords out of five utterly different timbres, and the only other time Mozart combined the flute with another wind instrument in chamber music was when he also employed the glass harmonica. The term 'wind quintet' suggests to lovers of classical music a work of very different calibre, namely, Mozart's glorious Quintet for piano, oboe, clarinet, horn, and bassoon. Beethoven's early and easy-going imitation of this is also well known, especially in his above-mentioned arrangement as a quartet for piano and strings. With Mozart the oboe leads, and with Beethoven the clarinet.

(*d*) Piano quintets, i.e. quintets for piano and string quartet, differ in no important aesthetic point from piano quartets. It is surprising how few have been written, and how abnormal is the position of those that are known as classics. Schubert's comparatively early *Forelle* Quintet (for pianoforte, violin, viola, violoncello, and double bass) is a voluminous and loose-knit serenade in five movements. Schumann's, the most popular of all, has, as already noted, no inner necessity to be written for a quintet rather than for a quartet or sextet or any larger combination. The masterpiece of Brahms, which sets a pure standard for the style, attained its final form only after a chequered existence,

c

first as a quintet for strings with two 'cellos, and then as a sonata for two pianos.

V. Sextets, &c.

(a) The two glorious masterpieces of Brahms for two violins, two violas, and two 'cellos are unmistakably inspired by the example of Schubert's great String Quintet.

(b) Octets for strings, i.e. four violins, two violas, and two 'cellos have tendencies to top-heaviness and internal congestion. Spohr accordingly hit upon the device of double quartets for two string quartet groups treated antiphonally. The genius of the boy Mendelssohn had, however, already discovered at the age of sixteen that two hundred and fifty odd antiphonal combinations are more interesting than Spohr's pair, and so he enjoyed himself without scruple in his Octet, and communicated his enjoyment to others.

(c) Most of the larger combinations of chamber music result from the grouping of strings with more than one wind instrument. The effect is often said to be semi-orchestral, but this is a mere illusion arising from the fact that wind instruments are seldom heard outside the orchestra, which they therefore suggest to the hearer. As a criterion, it is on a level with that of the backwoods critic who regretted that so superior a composition as Beethoven's op. 59, no. 1, had not been played by a larger band. The character of works like Beethoven's Septet and Schubert's glorification of the same scheme and combination as an octet (with the addition of a second violin) is neither orchestral nor hybrid, and in the one point where they differ from the purest chamber music, the introduction of the double-bass, the effect is essentially different from that of an orchestral bass. The style was perfectly understood by Mozart and Haydn, the Serenades and Divertimenti of Mozart being on every sort of scale, and sometimes for the queerest combinations. Such works are often voluminous, Beethoven's and Schubert's schemes of six movements with grand introductions to first movement and finale being typical, but the style is festive and the texture loose. In fact, the brilliant fixed contrasts of tone between the various instruments of these combinations go best with as light a style as the grand sonata forms will allow. The very terms serenade and divertimento suggest as much, and if the notion of chamber music is widened to tolerate the heavy-footed double bass, it may as well also allow the first violin to behave more like the solo instrument in a concerto than would be seemly in a string quartet.

(d) Compositions for wind instruments alone are most successful when pairs of each kind are taken, otherwise the balance of every chord is a *tour de force*. The greatest works in this line are

Mozart's two Octets for two oboes, two clarinets, two horns, and two bassoons. Both are entitled Serenades (like all Mozart's works for wind instruments alone), but the one in C minor is a grand and pathetic work, full of wonderful counterpoint and a most un-serenade-like seriousness. It is led throughout by the oboes, the tone of which becomes very fatiguing to the ear even with the finest playing. Perhaps this is why Mozart afterwards arranged it as a string quintet, in which form it is well known. The other octet is led by the clarinets and, though far slighter, can thus be far more easily produced. But the fact that Mozart is said to have first expanded it from a sextet by adding the oboes, and afterwards to have added two cors anglais, shows that we are leaving the region of a chamber music that tolerates no vagueness as to the number of players. The limit is reached in the same composer's glorious Serenade for two oboes, two clarinets, two basset horns (also clarinets), four horns, two bassoons, and contrafagotto or double bass.

Beethoven's works for wind instruments tell us only what he could learn from Mozart, and to pursue the subject into later times would be to lose our thread in a mass of detail.

After the Sonata Style

Wagner's revolution in the whole category of musical movement has had curiously little effect upon the forms of chamber music. One can only ascribe to pure formalism the way in which composers with atonal styles (like Ravel's) and perpetually modulating styles (like Reger's) cling to a set of forms and a group of four movements of which the sole meaning lies in propositions of classical key-relation and classical rapidity of action. There is a singular dearth of chamber music counterparts to the symphonic poem. The only general remark that is feasible here is that W. W. Cobbett's Phantasy prize-competitions have induced many of the best English composers of the twentieth century to relieve this dearth with a series of remarkable works in one continuous movement (with changes of tempo on original lines). For the rest, the tendencies of modern music are best discoverable by sympathetic accounts of the works of modern composers.

J. S. BACH

2. THE CLAVIERÜBUNG

(1936)

BACH's *Clavierübung* consists of four volumes of his ripest works, belonging to his later years in Leipzig and published by himself. Thus it not only represents his maturest musical thought, but is unique among his works in being presented to us in print with the author's final revisions. The vast bulk of Bach's work was not printed in his lifetime. Of more than two hundred Church cantatas only one, the quite early *Gott ist mein König* was printed, and estimates vary as to the number of choral works that are irrecoverably lost.

The title *Clavierübung* is in accordance with a custom not yet out of fashion in Bach's later days. It points to that healthy state of art in which there is no popular distinction between the academic exercise and the free art-form, nor between the amateur and the professional except when it was a question of choosing a master for an official post. Music, except for choral works on a large scale, was cultivated at home, and one reason why various beautiful early eighteenth-century instruments became obsolete was because they had not enough tone to be displayed in large rooms. The clavichord, the most sensitive of all Bach's keyed instruments, is scarcely, if at all, audible in public, and is, indeed, too delicate to be used in combination with any other instrument. Much has been dogmatically asserted as to which of Bach's works were written for the harpsichord and which for the clavichord. If there was any prospect of publishing keyboard music at all, no composer who hoped to sell his work would specify his keyed instruments more than could be helped. The *Clavierübung*, for instance, contains a volume of unequivocal organ music, and that explicitly liturgical; it contains three works, the 'Goldberg' Variations, the Italian Concerto, and the French Overture, which could not be played except on a harpsichord with two keyboards; and for the rest we may translate the word *Clavierübung* as 'keyboard-practice', and use the nearest available instrument. Similarly, Mr. Belloc called his first opus *The Bad Boy's Book of Beasts*, which nobly alliterative title was spoilt by the publisher, who pointed out that unless it was called *The Bad Child's Book of Beasts* its possible sales would be halved. Music that needs two keyboards and the various octave strings and stops of the harpsichord obviously cannot be played on the clavichord; but you can play clavichord music on the harpsichord at the sacrifice

20

of exquisite fine shades, but at the gain of broad contrasts and audibility at a distance. The clavichord leaves volume to the imagination and presents delicate shades of tone in reality. The harpsichord, with its organ-like capacity for doubling sounds in three octaves and for changing its qualities of tone, gives a quite satisfactory volume of sound and striking contrasts of colour, while it leaves finer shades to the imagination. In either case the imagination reacts to the suggestions made by the meaning of the music.

The 'Goldberg' Variations are not only thirty miracles of variation-form and counterpoint, but are a single miracle of consummate art as a whole composition. If the listener expects to recognize the air in the variations, either as a tune or as represented by its bass, he will misdirect his attention as fatally as if the statement that Michelangelo has a consummate grasp of anatomy were to lead him to study that master's work with an X-ray apparatus in one hand and a Quain's *Anatomy* in the other. A full analysis of the 'Goldberg' Variations is printed on pages 28–75 of this book.

I do not know any reason for distinguishing between a partita and a suite, unless it be that the title 'partita' seemed to Bach to allow more freedom than the title 'suite'; but even the partitas of Bach are far more faithful to the suite model than any suite by Handel, or, for that matter, by any other composer in whom I have been able to take an interest. I have never understood why my beloved master Parry seemed disturbed by the departures in these partitas from the precedents of Bach's two sets of suites known respectively as French and English. The deviations from type are too minute to concern any listener who is listening to music instead of collecting statistics.

The standard scheme of a suite consists of four essential movements, with the addition of one or more extras called *galanteries*. The essential movements are the allemande, the courante (or *corrente*), the sarabande, and the gigue. The *galanteries* are such things as the gavotte, the bourrée, and the minuet; often in pairs, of which in later times the second became designated as 'trio' from the fact that it was frequently in three-part harmony.

The allemande has no connexion with the lively *tedesca* known by that name to Beethoven. It is in moderate, or slow, common time, beginning with one or more notes before the first accent, and is normally a rather serious affair with a rich polyphonic texture. The graceful and fluent allemandes of the Sixth English Suite and the First Partita have become better known than any other specimens, but must not be taken as typical either in tempo or style.

There are two very different types of courante, and Bach has given us an equal number of examples of each. The French courante is a curiously abstruse affair, in a triple time which is just slow enough for its beats to be subdivided. Now, our everyday notion of triple time is more modern than most people realize. In the early eighteenth century the ordinary musical consciousness had not entirely forgotten the notion that the accentuation of six beats could swing from 2×3 to 3×2 without committing itself permanently to either. All Handel's triple-time cadences used this ambiguity, and Prout had the misfortune to quote, in a primer on composition, Handel's normal triple-time cadences as instances of faulty declamation. In most French courantes the time signature is three-two and the prevalent rhythm is true to it—that is to say, if you count six, you accentuate it: 1 2, 3 4, 5 6; but at the last bar of each section you will find that the accent is: 1 2 3, 4 5 6; and in many French courantes the two rhythms exist side by side elsewhere, sometimes one in the right hand and the other in the left. The French courantes have a tendency to dryness as well as abstruseness; but the specimen in the Fourth Partita is glorious and witty music, full of delightful melody with an evenly balanced conflict between the two opposing rhythms. The courantes in the Second Partitia and French Overture are slightly above the musical level of the courantes in the English Suites. The contrast between such a movement and the allemande is not great, and after an abstruse allemande a French courante adds little more than obscurity to the scheme.

The effect of an Italian courante is entirely different, being that of a continuously running movement in lively and unequivocal triple time. There are four Italian courantes in the French suites and four in the partitas. They all differ clearly from each other and from their surroundings. The magnificent courante in the Sixth Partita far transcends all others in scale and range of expression, as the allemande of the Fourth Partita transcends all other allemandes and is hardly to be compared with smaller things than a slow movement by Beethoven. One of the first things to be grasped about Bach's style, whether early or late, is that it is never more directly expressive than when it is most florid In the early days of the rediscovery of Bach his florid style was regarded as an obsolete fashion of his time. It was as much the fashion of any time as the vocabulary of Shakespeare; Bach was the sole master of it and he used it to express his deepest feelings.

The sarabandes of the six Partitas do not stand out conspicuously, as do the sarabandes of the French and English Suites. A typical sarabande is characterized by the rhythm: 1 2 3 & 1 2 3; where the small figures denote beats that are represented by pauses or rests. The most familiar of all sarabandes is the aria 'Lascia ch'io pianga La crude sorte' in Handel's *Rinaldo* known in some churches by its cruel maladjustment to the words 'O Lord rebuke me' (pause) 'not in Thine anger'. In the French and English Suites the sarabande has something of the weight and power of a central slow movement and its melody has breadth and simplicity. The sarabandes of the Partitas are more florid, and some of them retain hardly a trace of the original sarabande rhythm. In the third, fifth, and sixth Partitas, the sarabande does not even begin on the first of the bar, and some editors have even made the dreadful mistake of taking the sarabande of the Third Partita for a quick movement.

The *galanteries* are represented by one or two extra movements in each partita: a couple of minuets in the First; in the Second Partita by a rondeau of Couperin's form, which closely corresponds to the rondeau in verse, where the main theme is a single self-repeating phrase recurring after episodes which Couperin, following the example of the poets, calls *couplets*. In the Third Partita the sarabande is followed by a *burlesca* (miscalled minuet in some editions) and a scherzo. In the Fourth Partita an aria comes before the sarabande and a sturdy little minuet afterwards. The *galanteries* of the Fifth Partita consist of a 'tempo di menuetto' with a peculiar cross rhythm, certainly needing a double harpsichord to bring it out, and a passepied; the Sixth Partita has an air and a 'tempo di gavotta' after the sarabande. The airs in Bach's Suites are not, as you might expect, broad and simple melodies, but rather florid and fluent movements in a moderately quick tempo. The best-known, and the only slow one, is that in an orchestral suite which a vile custom has made familiar as an 'air on the fourth string', a transposition intended to produce a sonorous greasiness which would be greatly enhanced if violinists would kindly play it not only on one string but on one finger.

The gigues, or, as Bach and his editors often spelt them, 'giques', already show considerable variety in Bach's other suites, and the Partitas contain unique specimens. The most famous of all is the most individual. Being already in print in Bach's lifetime, its first twelve bars were transcribed unconsciously, but to an extent far beyond the possibility of coincidence, by a composer at the opposite pole of musical thought, Gluck, in the aria 'J'implore et je tremble', in *Iphigénie en Tauride*. It is curious to see how Gluck's rhetoric cannot attempt the subtlety with which Bach turns his climax into the dominant minor, a point which, even if it could 'get across the foot-lights', would confuse the simple emotions of Gluck's characters and situations. Otherwise this gigue, being entirely unpolyphonic, was easily absorbed into Gluck's aesthetic system. In the Second Partita the gigue is represented by a capriccio in duple time. The title shows that

Bach recognizes limits to the types of rhythm that can be associated with the gigue. Otherwise this capriccio resembles other
gigues, being practically a fugue fitted into the four-square
externals of a dance form, and with its subject turned upside-
down in the second half. The fact that the opening is accompanied need not prevent any one from recognizing the essentials
of fugue texture. In the other four partitas the gigues are in brilliant three-part fugue, either with inversion in the second half,
or with a new theme combining with the first theme. In the
Sixth Partita Bach, still writing in fugue form with inversion in
the second part, returns to an older type of gigue, not unlike the
Irish jig, in square time and jerky iambic rhythm.

The English Suites, the six Partitas, and the six Suites for
unaccompanied violoncello are enormously enlarged in their
scope by prefacing the set of dances with a short prelude. In
the Partitas each prelude has a special title. We need not trouble
to find a technical explanation of the difference between the
'praeludium' of the First Partita and the 'preambulum' of the
Fifth; nor need we inquire why the short slow introduction,
flowing andante, and quick two-part fugue of the Second Partita
should be called 'sinfonia'. The fantasia at the beginning of the
Third Partita is a much enlarged two-part 'invention', like the
four duets which have somehow crept into the volume of organ
chorales; but the overture of the Fourth Partita and the toccata
of the Sixth need more explanation. The overture is so-called
because, like the equally elaborate introduction to the isolated
B minor Partita known as the French Overture, it is in the form
which Lully initiated and Handel developed as the standard
orchestral introduction to an opera. You have first, in a rather
slow iambic rhythm, the solemn entry of the royalty and the
nobility, followed by a suitably lively and fugal 'tweedledee' of
His Majesty's fiddlers. Then, if, as was not unusual, the curtain
rose upon a ballet, your overture became a natural prelude to a
suite of dances. In the isolated French Overture and in Bach's
orchestral works, we also find a natural tendency for these dances
to consist mainly of the *galanteries*. The overture to the Fourth
Partita is one of Bach's greatest and most attractive examples.
Brahms, we may be sure, was not otherwise than delighted with
Bach's impudent prophetic plagiarism of the fugue-theme of the
allegro from the scherzo of Brahms's A major Pianoforte Quartet.

The toccata in the Sixth Partita shows very clearly the progress of Bach the improviser to Bach the perfecter of crystalline
musical form. A toccata is a 'touch-piece', idealizing the natural
habits of organists and harpsichord-players when they tried the
touch of their instruments. First, you must run about the keyboard and, as the case may be, the pedal-board, to see which of

the notes is unpunctual or out of action. Hence the idealization of jerky rhythms and surprising pauses in your rhapsodical opening. Then you must see, to quote Bach's own words, 'if your instrument has good lungs', and there will be a fine sonorous passage of sustained polyphony. When you are sure of your ground, you will then launch into the highest type of music, developed fugue, which will still retain in its themes a tendency towards jerky rhythms held together by sustained notes. The F sharp minor Toccata is a supremely beautiful example of Bach's earlier style. The toccata in the Sixth Partita shows how wonderfully he crystallizes the improvisatorial form into a design which, while not too symmetrical, gives an impression of absolute punctuality. The improvisatorial opening builds itself up into a four-square edifice with a flowing second theme which afterwards falls into place among the episodes of the very cogent and convincing fugue that follows. The fugue develops until we feel that, having heard what is evidently the first half of it, the whole must be going to be of enormous length. And here Bach shows us that, whatever notions we may have as to his tendency to crystallize his forms, he has lost none of his youthful freedom but has added power with responsibility. The rhapsodical opening returns in the dominant. Instead of becoming symmetrical, it expands until we gradually realize that the balance of key has swung round to our home tonic and that this expanded rhapsody is deliberately bringing the whole composition to an absolutely punctual end.

To Bach's contemporaries, playing on Bach's instruments, the titles of his works conveyed much more information about the proper way to play them than we are apt to recognize. Nobody could attempt to play the French Overture or the Italian Concerto on any instrument but a double harpsichord. Not only in the delightful Echo which ends the French Overture, but in many other prescriptions of *forte* in one hand and *piano* in the other, the harpsichord player could find unequivocal directions for about six differences of tone and volume; and the title of Italian Concerto could leave him in no possible doubt about his duty to indicate an orchestral tutti in the passages marked with a general *forte*, and a slow cantabile supported on a lute-like accompaniment when the right hand was *forte* and the left *piano*. The Italian Concerto is one of the most familiar of Bach's clavier works, and its perfection of form and clearness of matter has made it intelligible in spite of pianistic traditions which horribly mutilate every feature of its true lines.

Apart from the four duets, and framed by the grand E flat Prelude and Fugue for full organ, the third book of the *Clavierübung* consists of a set of twenty-one organ chorales, containing the severest, but also some of the grandest, music that Bach ever wrote. All the chorales have two settings, one for full organ with pedals and the other on a smaller scale for manuals alone. The *Gloria, Allein Gott in der Höh' sei Ehr*, has three settings. I do not advise the listener to expect more from the music than what would engage my own attention—that is, a flow of noble fugue texture dominated by the choral tune entering at intervals phrase by phrase in long notes in the treble or the bass or an inner part. Bach calls the dominating tune the canto fermo, and on the organ the mere length of its notes distinguishes it well enough from the surrounding counterpoints.

The smaller settings are mostly short fugues on themes suggested by the first line of the chorale. If we to-day knew the chorale-tunes as well as Bach's congregation knew them we might appreciate the cross-word wit of the derivation. But it is immaterial to our enjoyment of these fughettas as music.

The chorales concern the central doctrines of the Church, and are to some extent parallel with those of the Mass. The ground covered includes that of the *Kyrie, Gloria*, and *Credo*; with the Ten Commandments, the Lord's Prayer, Baptism, and the doctrine of Atonement (corresponding to the *Agnus Dei*). Most of the tunes are derived from Gregorian music, with the character of the Church modes strongly marked. You must not be surprised if your ordinary notions of key are contradicted; nor, on the other hand, must you expect that text-book information about the Church modes will help you any more than the Englisshe of Ye Olde Furniture Shoppe will help you to understand Shakespeare.

The canto fermo of the full organ settings of the *Kyries* is a three-fold Gregorian tone in the Phrygian mode, that is to say, in a scale of white notes ranging from E to E. Church modes will seem most intelligible to you if you take their scales downwards, so that your standard Phrygian scale is E D C B A G F E. These three chorales being pitched a third higher, their scale is G F E flat D C B flat A flat G; and the impression of key is that of a mixture of the dominant of E flat gravitating towards the dominant of C minor. But when the canto fermo is in an inner part the end may just as well become a tonic chord of C major.

The Mixolydian mode (a white-note scale from G to G) is shown in *Dies sind die heil'gen zehn Gebot*. A majestic and elaborate duet on one manual deals with several original and florid themes, while pedal supplies a solid foundation. The canto fermo is a tune with the archaic severity of a Gregorian tone, and is given in canon by two middle parts, led sometimes by the lower voice and sometimes by the upper.

The version for manuals only is a four-part fugue on the first line of the chorale with no canto fermo. As that line consists mainly of repeated notes, its transformation into a lively fugue-subject in 12/8 time, with intervening skips and a flowing continuation, leaves us with a piece of music which we need not burden with doctrinal import: otherwise we might question the orthodoxy of treating the Ten Commandments by inversion. But Bach is only anticipating Haydn's apology for the indecorum of 'worshipping God with a cheerful heart'.

The fugue-subject of *Wir glauben all' an einen Gott* (full organ) is a quick-time syncopated version of the first line of the tune. At first there is no main beat for the syncopation to lean against, so the rhythm does not reveal itself until the harmony is complete. The striding recurring theme of the pedal has given rise to the title of 'The Giant', by which this piece is known. There is no canto fermo until the end, where the second line of the tune appears in the tenor.

In the first version of *Christ unser Herr zum Jordan kam* the main figure of the counterpoint is suggested by the first line of the tune, imitating a river of sound. Doubtless many other details in the counterpoint may be traced to graphic or doctrinal origins; but the music is clear enough without research into such things. The mode turns out to be Phrygian. I am unable to trace much symbolism in any of the other twenty chorales. This is the more remarkable in the case of *Jesus Christus unser Heiland*, because one of the most beautiful of Bach's earlier settings of *Jesus Christus* is the *locus classicus* for a clear and beautifully musical symbolism of each line of the text: the wrath of God needing the sacrifice of the Mediator, the sufferings of Christ, and the joy of Paradise finally secured for sinful mortals.

The pedal version of *Vater unser im Himmelreich* is perhaps the most difficult of all Bach's chorales, not because of its elaborate scheme, but because of its enormous wealth of expressive detail. Bach has taken exceptional pains to make it sound clear by means of slurs and staccato marks, so that the florid parts may not become confused with the double canto fermo which has to be played on the same manuals. The scheme is like that of the great setting of *Dies sind die heil'gen zehn Gebot*: that is to say, there are a fugued duet for a treble and alto, an independent bass for pedals, and the canto fermo is given phrase by phrase in canon for two other voices. The obstacles to clearness consist, first, in the fact that the free duet is based on a florid version of the first line of the canto fermo in the same tempo, and secondly that it is impossible to put the canonic canto fermo on a separate manual. But the whole is profoundly beautiful in conception.

The two settings of *Aus tiefer Noth* are my favourite illustrations of the ideal relations between form and matter. What is form and what is matter, when the canto fermo is given to the composer, and some seventy per cent. of the whole setting is accounted for by the statement that the other parts are dealing with each phrase successively by fugue in contrary motion? The result is a beautiful piece of musical rhetoric. Could we conceive that the rhetoric was the composer's pre-established condition, or 'form', and that the crystalline accuracy of the counterpoint was the 'matter'? As a practical proposition the idea seems absurd, but as a theory of art not only are matter and form thus interchangeable, but, in the case of the tune itself, the rhetoric did actually come first, for the tune was made to illustrate the metrical version of *De Profundis*.

3. ARIA WITH THIRTY VARIATIONS (THE 'GOLDBERG' VARIATIONS) (1900)

INTRODUCTION

The Vitality of Artistic Counterpoint, and the Possibilities of the Harpsichord

THIS work is often described as the 'Goldberg' Variations, after a famous pupil for whom Bach wrote them. Goldberg was a great harpsichord player, whose patron, Count Kayserling, suffered greatly from neuralgia, and commissioned Bach to write a work sufficiently voluminous and interesting to divert his mind during his long sleepless nights. Bach succeeded not only in producing one of the greatest works of art ever written for a single instrument, but also in delighting the suffering Count. 'Dear Goldberg, please come and play me my Variations,' became a frequent request from the invalid; and Bach was rewarded not only with the evident affection the Count showed for his work, but also with a golden goblet containing one hundred Louis-d'or: probably the highest payment he ever received for any single composition.

The 'Goldberg' Variations are still often mentioned, but seldom given their due. No treatise on counterpoint is complete without extracts from their 'canons', and no disquisition on variations as an art form can dispense with a reference to them as one of the two greatest sets of variations ever written—the second being Beethoven's Thirty-three on a Waltz of Diabelli, and no other set being even half so voluminous. Yet it may be doubted whether any other great classic is really so little known as regards essentials, or so liable to grotesque misrepresentation. The very features that are most frequently quoted are misinterpreted as the most serious obstacles against a wider and more popular understanding of the work. Every third variation is a canon; these canons are arranged in arithmetical order of interval; and the canon-form is, in weak hands, a mechanically rigid and academic one. Therefore, it is frequently concluded that these canons are mechanical, and that the work is disorganized by their regular occurrence at each third variation.

At the present day, the crudities of those elementary technical makeshifts which are sometimes falsely called 'academic principles' have provoked an equally crude reaction against everything that happens to interest those artists who know the technique of their art. It sometimes seems as if the surest way to damage the reputation of a work is to show that its structure is ingenious beyond the reach of amateurish plodding. Certainly some such condition of things is the only possible explanation of the widespread idea that the canons in the 'Goldberg' Variations are a technical *tour de force* carried through at the expense of pure musical interest. Apart from the simple expedient of bringing the whole glorious work to a hearing, there is only one way to meet such fallacies, and that is by showing how ubiquitous these ingenious contrapuntal devices are in all great music—how even a composer like Schubert, notoriously weak in academic technique, shows a profound feeling for their essential principles and characteristics, just in his most poetical and impressive passages; and how Mozart in such light-hearted movements as the finale of the D major Quintet has designed all his themes to combine in quadruple counterpoint, and in general makes his finales and developments move in counterpoint in as many parts as his instruments can produce without losing a firm harmonic basis.

As for Bach, if he had chosen to label the canons in his other works as he has labelled those in the great variations, those of us who distrust contrapuntal skill would long ago have concluded that he never wrote any genuine music at all. The third movement of the A major Violin Sonata has always been regarded as one of the most directly expressive and melodious utterances of the eighteenth century: there was once a time when it would not have been thought unfashionable to compare it to a Mendelssohn 'Song Without words'. Yet it is in strict canon from the first note to the last, and is at least three times as long as any of the canons in the 'Goldberg' Variations. Or, again, to turn to his best-known choral work, the 'Qui tollis' of the B minor Mass is not a movement which any critic or student has yet accused of 'academic stiffness'; yet in it the voices proceed in four-part canon at various intervals, while the wind instruments accompany with a largely independent two-part canon, and all this for at least as long a time as any of these 'Goldberg' canons.

The truth is that it is no more exceptional for Bach to write in
canon, whether strict or free, than it is for a poet to write in
verse. It is by no means unnecessary to insist on this, for any
mischief that may have been done by the ineptitudes of pseudo-
academic contrapuntists is but dust in the balance against the
loss of enjoyment and deadening of intellect that result from
crude anti-academic strictures on the methods of classical art.
The non-technical lover of art suffers perhaps more from the
spread of such notions than the half-instructed spreaders of
them, for he would never be disturbed by the fact that a beautiful
piece of tranquil melodic weaving like the ninth 'Goldberg'
Variation (Canone alla Terza) had a rigid mechanical principle
in its structure, if he did not constantly hear such terms as
'canonic', 'academic', and 'contrapuntal' coupled with the
epithets 'crabbed', 'mechanical', &c. Another danger arising
from this prejudice is that as the 'Goldberg' canons, like all
complex parts of a great work of art, do contain here and there
a difficult and surprising harmony or turn of phrase, we may be
predisposed to regard these incidents as defects resulting from
the mechanical structure, instead of treating them with the
respectful consideration we pay to precisely similar things in
works which we do not know to be canons. For example, the
following passage in the twenty-first variation:

Ex. 1

with its strange skips of 7ths at *, * and its still stranger harmony
at the second of the two skips, may easily be mistaken by a
prejudiced mind for a sacrifice of musical sense to the exigencies
of a mechanical 'canon in the 7th'. How false such an idea really
is may be seen from the fact that the passage could easily be
altered, as follows:

Ex. 2

which is just as strict canon, and just as faithful to the theme. But with all its smoothness and obviousness it is very far from being either as rich or as natural as the original.

Whatever Bach's motives, then, for strange progressions and harsh inversions, they have nothing to do with the mechanical exigencies of canon-writing; for any contrapuntist of moderate skill could 'correct' them on the above model without loss of canonic strictness. They are on precisely the same purely aesthetic footing as the abrupt inversions and strange figures that we find in the poetry of Virgil and Milton. To sum up, in the criticism of any highly organized work of art it is very dangerous to make any *a priori* strictures from ingenuities, alleged or real, in technical structure. No artist capable of producing a large work at all would destroy its unity by such a childish mistake as the insertion of passages constructed on technical principles he had so little mastered that every critic and every dilettante could detect his weakness at once. When strictures on an elaborate work are so easy that a child can make them off-hand, that is the strongest evidence that they are wrong.

This does not mean that there are no works by great artists in which abstract technicalities are not cultivated regardless of pure artistic results; nor does it mean that there are not in existence certain contrapuntal and other technical problems which will probably never be solved by higher than mechanical methods. But in the works of great artists such matters generally stand self-confessed, and, in spite of much actual artistic interest, openly disclaim artistic unity. *Die Kunst der Fuge* is not even written for an assigned combination of instruments or voices. The purely ingenious portion of *Das Musikalische Opfer* is confined to two pages of canons which, so far from masquerading as music, are written in an enigmatic form, while the rest of the work is not only among Bach's highest and purest art, but has less definitely academic technique in it than most of his work at the same period. And the Variations on *Vom Himmel hoch*, which he wrote as a demonstration of his contrapuntal skill, are entitled *Einige canonische Veränderungen*, &c., which obviously implies that they are not intended to form a connected whole.

The contrast between these cases and that of the 'Goldberg' Variations is manifest at a glance. In the latter, everything points to the supreme importance of the unity of the work as a thing to be played and heard in its entirety. After the last variation we find the direction 'Aria Da Capo', which tells us, before we have verified its effect, that Bach intends his work to be rounded off by making it end as it began. Then, the directions 'a 1 Clav' or 'a 2 Clav', which we find at the head of each variation, show not only that Bach was writing for a harpsichord with two manuals, but that he was unusually anxious that the player should use both manuals together at the appropriate passages—for there are, at least, three variations headed 'a 2 Clav' which would be quite as easy to play on one manual; and in no other clavier-work does Bach trouble to make such indications, though he frequently wrote for a double-manual harpsichord. Bach is, then, writing here with even more than his usual attention to the circumstances of actual performance.

This leads us to another important subject, the differences between the harpsichord and the modern pianoforte. These are by no means entirely to the advantage of the latter; and it is surprising how a little acquaintance with the former enlarges our ideas of the range and brilliance of Bach's compositions for it. The harpsichord, though far inferior to the pianoforte in cantabile expression, power, and variety, yet had capabilities in view of which the adequate performance of harpsichord music on the modern pianoforte becomes a larger problem than it is often supposed to be. Nothing, for instance, is farther from the truth than the idea that all harpsichord music should be played on the pianoforte with great uniformity of expression and a small tone. It is true that the actual volume of sound produced by a large harpsichord is by no means great; but the ear does not judge by mere volume, it rather measures its impressions by the evident capacity of the instrument. The loudest fortissimo of a pianoforte would hardly hold its own against the mezzo-forte of a full orchestra; but if a musician were to arrange a pianoforte work for full orchestra, he would not on that account turn all the fortissimos into mezzo-fortes, though he might well take advantage of the orchestra's greater range of tone and use more gradations than he found in the original composition. But where in the original the single instrument obviously plays its loudest, there in the arrangement the orchestra must also obviously play its loudest, or it will give an utterly misleading impression.

On the other hand the harpsichord, though no more sensitive to 'touch' than the organ, had, like the organ, stops by which the player could obtain many varieties both in quantity and quality of tone. Some harpsichords, mostly English, had also a 'Venetian Swell' covering the strings and opening and shutting like a Venetian blind to let the sound issue in greater or less fulness, producing a very recognizable crescendo or diminuendo. Bach's harpsichord had no Venetian Swell, but it had more stops than most of the English specimens, possessing 16-foot, as well as 4- and 8-foot registers. To show what this means, I cannot do better than quote the beginning of the 'Italian' Concerto as Bach probably made it sound. He writes thus:

Ex. 3

As he is avowedly imitating the opening tutti of a concerto with orchestra, there can be no manner of doubt that he intends this to be given with the full power of the instrument, playing on the lower manual (as an organist would play on the 'great organ') and drawing his 4- and 16-foot registers. The result will be as follows, and very rich and thrilling too:

Ex. 4

Hence it has sometimes been argued that we ought frequently to add octaves in playing harpsichord music on the pianoforte; but this seems, on nearer examination, fallacious. There is a world of difference between octaves produced once for all by a mechanical agency and octaves produced by the special application of a finger to each note as required. In the former case the sensation of octaves is almost immediately lost in a feeling of mere increase in brilliance or depth of tone, whereas in the latter the ear never loses its consciousness that the notes are actually doubled. In the above example, before the listener had heard beyond the second bar his general impression would be that the real notes were those of the middle octave to which the lower octave was giving a depth of tone which would predominate but for the counterbalancing brilliance of the highest octave. No such impression could be given by playing all these doublings note for note on the modern pianoforte; we should only feel that the part-writing (a matter of paramount importance in Bach) was obscured, and all possibility of really free and natural phrasing lost.

The nearest possible translation from the language of the harpsichord to that of the modern pianoforte is here, as in almost all cases, to play the music exactly as it is written, but to use the

D

whole fulness of tone that one's fingers can produce. The genius of the pianoforte is to make gradations and 'colours' of tone by touch; the genius of the harpsichord is to do the same by 4- and 16-foot registers, 'lute stops', and the like; deficiencies in the finer details of cantabile expression being supplied by the imagination of the sympathetic listener (for in those days listeners were few, but always sympathetic and imaginative, because they generally made music in private or in church, and did not regard the public concert as the normal vehicle of musical utterance). The pianoforte leaves some things to the imagination, but the finer details of cantabile expression are not among these things; and the imagination utterly refuses to supply a deficiency which it perfectly well knows is not inherent in the instrument. Therefore, so long as we avoid weak or exclusively modern traits, so long as we do not indulge in unscholarly renderings of ornaments, in pedal effects based on modern conceptions antagonistic to distinct part-writing, in sophistications, paradoxes, flippancy, *Weltschmerz*, and all else that makes art unnecessarily hard to understand, we cannot put too much life into our reading of old classics.

It is still fashionable to call Bach 'severe'; but the term, doubtless a correct one, has come to have a curious special sense. The 'severe' artist seems, when we come to know him, to be a man who can obtain from the simplest and most obvious things more enjoyment for himself and others than the ordinary artist can obtain from the most extravagant modern resources. What is the technical staple of these 'Goldberg' Variations? Counterpoint—an art so simple that we teach it to our musical students several years before we undertake to help in their experiments in the simplest forms of composition. What means has Bach for bringing his great set of variations to an end that shall seem really final? None whatever except the grouping and contrasting of the variations themselves, and the simple repetition of the original theme after the last variation. What is the harmonic range of the work? Simply that of the theme, plus such addition as is inevitable when translating its harmonies into a minor key. What is the rhythmic range? In grouping of bars the rhythm is always exactly that of the theme, but in time and beats all the variations differ. These narrow limitations, then, should give a 'severe' character to the work; and yet in the ordinary sense of the word, this would only be so if they really seemed to hamper the composer where he might otherwise have indulged in wit, brilliance, pathos, and what not. But, so far from this being the case, Bach has never covered so wide a range of feeling and effect in any other instrumental work. Looking at it in its least severe aspect we are at once brought face to face with the undoubted fact that until Beethoven wrote the 'Waldstein' Sonata, the 'Goldberg' Variations were the most brilliant piece of sheer instrumental display extant. No other work by Bach himself, or by Domenico Scarlatti, not even any concerto by Mozart or any earlier work of Beethoven could compare with it for instrumental brilliance. Again, take its range of feeling. The twenty-fifth variation is one of the saddest strains ever penned. The thirtieth is a 'Quodlibet', a contrapuntal hotch-potch of snatches of popular songs— songs of which the titles and first words are known, so that, apart from the undeniably rollicking character of the tunes themselves, we have no possible doubt that Bach is writing in a mood which an ordinary modern composer would be likely to regard as one of dangerous high spirits rather than one sufficiently severe for the production of a great and serious work.

Let us now examine this severe work as a whole, with so much the greater courage since it would seem, if we may judge by the simplicity of Bach's resources and the range and depth of his feeling, that the severe artist is, after all, a man with an enviably simple capacity for enjoying life.

ANALYSIS

A glance at the theme will show that, whatever else Bach may intend to make the underlying principle of his variations, the melody is not the essential point. The first four bars of the melody, quoted below, are already so crowded with ornaments that the only conceivable way to make melodic variations on such a theme would be to do as Handel has done in his D minor Suite, and *simplify* the melody while varying the accompaniment. This plan is only suitable for very small and simple sets of variations; and we shall find that in the present work the melody of the theme, fine and graceful as it is, has nothing whatever to do with the variations. Indeed, if we examine it closely we shall find that it could not be simplified like Handel's ornate D minor theme; all Bach's arabesques (except the mere mordents and shakes) are essential to the melodic sense.

Nor is it rhythm and structure that Bach can take as the basis of his variations. The theme is 32 bars long, subdivided into two 16-bar sections, four 8-bar sub-sections, eight 4-bar phrases, and (if we like to push the matter to the end) sixteen 2-bar clauses. This rigid regularity gives no hold for a variation to establish itself on rhythmic principles; nor do we find anything definite enough in the smaller details of rhythm inside the bars. There is nothing there but an elusive impression of the characteristic sarabande rhythm—

Ex.5

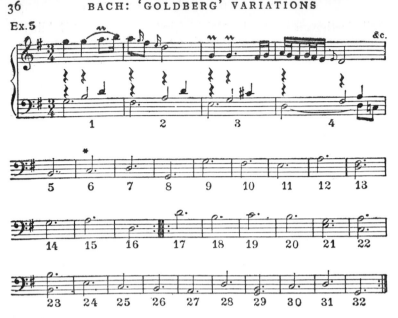

* After the sixth bar I have given the bass, not as it actually occurs in the theme or in any new variation, but as it is in essentials, as determined by taking its average in all the variations. The reader will readily understand that even in the theme it is often filled out with a good deal of movement between its main steps. Hence the double notes here and there in the above digest.

giving elasticity and organization to the elaborate stream of ornamentation above, but not itself clearly recognized. Indeed, the one variation where this rhythm is clearly brought out, the twenty-sixth, is as sharply contrasted with the theme as any, and in no way recalls its rhythm to us more than the other variations.

It is to the bass that we must look for our guiding lines, and so I quote here only the first four bars of the theme in full, continuing with the bass alone.

Now, there are two ways of regarding such a bass as this. We may take it as a bass in the melodic sense; that is, as a melody placed in the lowest part. For example, we may regard the first four bars as a descending scale from G to D, and reproduce it in the following form, with strange new harmonies above it, as Bach does throughout the twenty-fifth variation:

Ex.6

Or we may regard it as representing harmony, and reproduce its harmony without its melodic outline, as in Variation 10, where these first four bars are represented by the subject of a little fugue that accurately represents the harmonies, though the sense of steady descent from G to D is almost entirely lost:

Ex. 7

Or these two methods may be inextricably blended, and both of them treated with considerable latitude, as in the ninth variation an extraordinary case quoted by Parry in the splendid article 'Variations', in Grove's *Dictionary of Music and Musicians*. This passage, and others like it, we may reserve for discussion when we reach them in the ordinary course of our analysis. At present it will be enough to say that the actual principles of Bach's variation-making (*qua* variation) are simple enough; and that, once we grasp the fact that it is a bass and harmonic scheme, not a melody and rhythmic scheme, that he is varying, whatever difficulties the 'Goldberg' Variations may give us will not be matters of variation-technique. Our task is now to analyse the variations as individual forms, and to trace their development, not from the thematic standpoint, but from that of mood, contrast, and climax.

The first variation at once leaves the mood and texture of the theme. It is a duet between the right hand and the left, the hands having different material, which they interchange phrase by phrase:

Ex. 8

The steps of the bass are very clearly the same as in the theme. In the second quatrain of bars the two hands change parts, the right having figure (*b*) and the left (*a*). At the ninth bar (beginning the second sub-section) a new idea appears in combination with a variant of (*b*):

Ex. 9

At the thirteenth bar the left hand treats this new figure freely by inversion, the right having, as before, something akin to the left hand's former material:

Ex. 10

(c) inverted

The second half of the variation is on the same lines as the first, but not exactly so. The extreme regularity of the theme, with its thirty-two bars always divided by twos and fours, and the absolute necessity of preserving this rhythm through all the variations, make Bach avoid anything like a similar rigidity in the distribution of his figures. I have analysed this first variation somewhat minutely, because it will serve, once for all, as the type of the many duet-variations we shall come to in the course of the work. With only two exceptions all the duet-variations are like the first, brilliant pieces of instrumental writing, giving the two hands differentiated material, and at every four-bar phrase either making the hands change parts, or inverting the figures, or introducing a fresh idea.

The wide arpeggios and leaps of the first variation, together with its obvious twofold intention as a contrast to the theme and as a beginning of a great and vigorous artistic process, all point to its being meant to be full and rich in tone. In the second variation we see the reaction from this outburst of vigour. The time changes from triple to duple; instead of runs, arpeggios, and skips, we have smooth cantabile outlines; and the structure shows us a second type, the variation being a trio. In this trio, as in many subsequent ones in the work, the two upper parts are in imitative dialogue, while the bass, at some distance below, weaves different matter round the steps of the theme, only occasionally using the figures of the upper parts.

Ex. 11

&c.

Note how the composite figure (*c*), which in the fifth bar needs two parts to express it, becomes in the eighth bar a single figure and approximate to figure (*b*) in effect. In the second part, these figures (*a*), (*b*), and (*c*) become more intimately blended, and the bass takes its share in their treatment.

Ex. 12

I put the two upper parts on separate staves because they cross in such an intricate way. The last section of the variation, which contains its finest sequence, is so closely interwoven that I here disentangle the two upper parts throughout the last nine bars:

Ex. 13

Here, as before, a detailed analysis of this first specimen of a definite type helps us to understand, once for all, how later variations of the same type are constructed. The next variation is the first of the series of Canons, and these are, with the exception of that in the ninth, simply variations of the type just analysed, except that the relation of the upper parts is, so to speak, crystallized; that is to say, if we suppose the second variation so altered that one of the two upper parts echoes its fellow note instead of merely sharing its material, then we shall have a canon on precisely the same lines as eight of the nine existing canons. The relation of the bass to the upper parts, at firss independent, but showing a tendency to share their material at the variation proceeds; the subtle and epigrammatic treatment of figures; and the frequent and complex crossing of the upper parts, so strongly thrown into relief by the distance they almost always keep between themselves and the bass; all these characteristics of the second variation are also found in the canons, so that we may regard the second variation not only as a contrast to the first, but as a preparation for the canons, it being the only one of its type that is not actually canonic.

The third variation is by far the most difficult of the canons. Bach has cunningly devised the last line of the second variation to prepare the ear for the extraordinary crossing of parts which characterizes his first canon. I here disentangle the entire first half of the variation; in the second half the parts stand out much more simply (see pp. 41–42).

But far more subtle than the canonic structure and crossing of parts are Bach's treatment of the harmonic basis, and his motive for the freedom he there adopts. The numerals here given below the bass correspond with those in Ex. 1; and comparison will prove that Bach's apparent freedom in this third variation is the result of a definite artistic principle. At the outset half a bar of the variation corresponds with a whole bar of the theme, the steps in the bass being quite clearly reproduced. This average of rhythmic relationship is faithfully maintained throughout the variation as far as the length of its whole sections is concerned; but soon after the entry of the answer the harmonies are made to crowd in prematurely, and the time thus gained is filled out by repeating them. Bach's motives are clear; he wishes the canon to be heard by the ear, not merely studied by the contrapuntal student's eye. He wishes this variation not only to be a beautiful and characteristic canon in the unison, but to owe its beauty and character to the fact that it is a canon in the unison. The canonic parts cross so much just because they are in exactly the same position; and the harmonies are made to repeat themselves because by so doing they emphasize the fact that the answer echoes the subject. Having thus thrown into relief the most characteristic features of canon in unison, Bach devotes the second part of the variation to developing some fresh features. If the canonic parts can be kept distinct, it is very effective to harmonize the answer differently from the subject. In the wonderful canonic Andante of the A major Violin Sonata, Bach does this almost throughout, but in this case the subject and answer are on two different instruments, so that the canon is self-evident no matter how it is constructed. In the 'Goldberg' Variations the canons are on one instrument, and that one with very limited power of 'phrasing', so that Bach was wise in using strange means to express the essential nature of his canon at the

Ex. 14

outset, reserving this more attractive device for the second part. The second part is, accordingly, much easier to follow than the first; and the bass is more nearly that of the theme, though towards the end some more crowding and repetition appears—coinciding as before with complex crossing of the upper parts.

The first three variations have all been in more or less long bars, so that the harmonic steps have moved somewhat slowly, even in the half-bars of the third variation. With the fourth variation we have (as with all until the twenty-ninth) another change of time, but in this case it is not felt so much as such, since it is a triple rhythm in nearly the same tempo as the 12/8 beats of the preceding variation. On the other hand, the change is felt in a much fresher and deeper way as one from slow to quick successions of harmony. With these short 3/8 bars the harmony changes after every three notes, thus causing the variation to run its course very tersely, even if played with all the repeats.[1]

The variation is again of a fresh type, four-part polyphonic treatment of a single figure, here treated directly and inverted:

Ex.15

&c.

* Throughout the musical examples ⌢a⌝ indicates the direct figure; ⌄a⌝ its inversion. Here the latter soon crowds out the direct figure altogether.

The harmonies and bass are very close to the theme, thus enhancing the contrast this variation with its full four-part harmony already makes with the preceding. It contains few notes that are not either the little group of three that (mostly inverted) forms its text, or else part of the bass of the theme, which bass we will henceforth call the Base (so spelled, and with a capital B).

The fifth variation is of the first type, as we saw in the first variation, a brilliant duet. Though its material differentiates and develops as it proceeds, we cannot, as in the first variation, trace

[1] I must here take the opportunity of explaining my treatment in performance of the repeats, which Bach indicates indiscriminately throughout the whole work. It would be not only tedious but very unscholarly to play them all, for in Bach's time repeat-marks were still largely used as a conventional companion to the double-bar, involving no obligation on the player to repeat unless he chose. On the other hand, balance and expression alike render it out of the question to omit all the repeats, and I select some ten or twelve variations as necessarily to be played with repeats on some or other of the following grounds, viz.: clearness (e.g., Var. 3), short bars (Vars. 4, 10, 18, 19, 22), isolation (Var. 21), and climax (the last three Variations).

two distinct pairs of themes. The initial pair is the only one that needs quotation:

Ex. 16

Harmonies and Base are very clear. In this variation we see the first signs of the use Bach makes of his double keyboard. He heads the variation 'a 1 ovvero 2 clav', but a harpsichord player would soon hasten to use both manuals, for Bach already indulges in passages where the hands would collide very inconveniently on a single keyboard. On the pianoforte such passages are easy enough to express by dint of phrasing, light touch, accent, and special redistribution; but on the unresponsive harpsichord the independence given by a second keyboard is absolutely necessary.

The sixth variation is the canon in the second; and, as before, Bach takes good care that it shall derive its most characteristic effects from the fact that it is a canon in the second. We are most of us familiar with the beautiful pleading, surging effect of the canonic sequences with which Pergolesi's *Stabat Mater*—

Ex. 17

and the 'Recordare' of Mozart's *Requiem* begin:

Ex. 18

The effect is one that can only be produced by canon in the second. No other intervals, except the seventh and ninth, can produce the strong but easily resolved discord with which each bar of this type of passage begins; and these are too wide an interval to produce the characteristic crossing of parts. And unless the passage is canonic, and the answer in the upper part, we cannot obtain that doubling of the steps of rising sequence by which the peculiarly insistent effect is produced.

Bach begins his canon with the effect of entering on a suspended discord—

Ex. 19

but reserves the effect of crossing parts and rising sequences for the next sub-section (bars 9–16), an exquisite passage, worthy to rank with the wonderful opening of Mozart's 'Recordare', as an example of the power of expression which strict canon sometimes can give:

Ex. 20

The bass seems at first sight more free than it really is. Bach is reproducing not his thematic Base, but the principal harmonics. The actual bass of this variation is organized on the principle of making rising sequences wherever possible, and always touching something corresponding to the original harmony or Base-note, though not necessary on the first beat of the bar. Only at the two principal cadences does Bach make a real change, and that is the very happy and rich one of substituting an analogous chromatic Base (G, G♯, A, D, and the corresponding notes in the second part) for the original diatonic Base (F♯, G, A, D). (See bars 13–16 and 29–32.)

In the second part note the happy chromatic variation in the initial figure, and the new rising and crossing sequence towards the end, so finely thrown into relief by the stopping of the semiquaver flow in the bass, and the strong falling sevenths which appear instead.

The seventh variation is a duet, but of a type which does not occur elsewhere in the work. It is a delightfully graceful and attractive little gigue, containing (like most of the other **duets**) two pairs of themes:

Ex. 21

The Base and harmonies are quite simply represented.

The eighth variation is again a very brilliant duet of the first type; in which the initial pair of figures—

Ex. 23

alternates with its inversion (in both members)—

Ex. 24

and with a combination of (*a*) and a new figure—

Ex. 25

Before long (*a*) is given simultaneously **direct and inverted,**

with the result that the hands, starting some distance apart, soon meet and cross in such a way that the player has no difficulty in understanding why Bach marks this variation 'a 2 Clav'.

As in all the duet variations, except the anomalous canon in the ninth, Base and harmonies are quite simply reproduced.

The ninth variation is the canon in the third, and here Bach brings out quite a new result from this fact. The canonic parts are still close enough to cross frequently; but, in sharp contrast to the energy and bustle of the eighth variation, Bach secures a smooth and luxuriously drooping effect by avoiding dissonances and assigning the answer to the lower of the two canonic parts. The result of this is that when (as in the canon in the second) he makes the parts cross in dovetailed sequence, all the sequences fall (since the answer is lower than the subject), and then the subject can cross the answer only by going below it, thus driving the answer lower still. Also the resulting sequential steps are steps of a third, which is a larger interval than a second; so that these falling sequences are on a larger scale than the rising sequences of the canon in the second.

Here is the beginning of the variation, showing a remarkable development in the treatment of the bass:

Ex.26 ✲✲

** Half-bars correspond to whole bars of the theme; at the third half-bar Bach interprets the original Base—a descent from G to D, as a *rise* from G to D and then, as Parry points out in *Grove*, continues with an ascending passing-note (✲) instead of the descending passing-note of bar 4 of the theme; thus

As in the canon in the second, Bach does not begin crossing parts at once, but in the third bar we see the beautiful falling sequences appear. The harmony is very smooth until the middle of the second half, where the increasing complexity seems, as it were, to press one strangely expressive dissonance from the harmonic flow.

The tenth variation is of the third type; full four-part polyphonic treatment of a figure, such as we have already seen once in the fourth variation. But here the form is crystallized into a complete little fughetta. The fugue-subject (no mere short figure, but a whole four-bar phrase) I have already quoted in No. 3, as an illustration of Bach's representation of the Base by harmonies instead of by steps. By one or the other it is simply and clearly represented throughout; and if we look back we shall see that so far Bach has worked on a very artistic principle as to the placing and contrasting of his canons and their sequels. He has given the canons considerable latitude as to details of harmony and bass, partly, as we have seen, on principles that help to bring out the characteristics of canonic structure, but also with the purpose of counteracting, by freedom in other respects, any mechanical or crudely academic effect that such strict and clearly marked canons might otherwise produce. This being so, he has in all three cases followed them by variations that are strict in harmony, clear in texture, and very definite in theme, with no rapid or dazzling motion. And after these he further clears the air with a brilliant instrumental duet, as we shall see again in Variation 11. To return to the fughetta; it pushes clearness to an effective extreme. The theme (quoted in No. 3) enters with amusing regularity after every four bars, accommodating itself to the harmonies of the theme or Base. In the first half the four voices enter in the order—bass, tenor, soprano, and alto; in the second part this order is exactly reversed as regards pitch, thus—soprano, alto, bass, tenor. The variation makes a most effective climax to the first stage of our journey in Bach's great variation-world—and we will pause here while I take the reader into my confidence about a quaint little piece of musical lumber I happen to possess: a strange and, to the best of my belief, quite unknown result of this wonderful work.

The name of Johann Nicolaus Forkel is still remembered as that of the earliest biographer of Bach. That Forkel was also a

---

leading to the intrusion of a fresh chord (†) and crowding the other harmonies into close quarters. Afterwards he makes the bass repeat itself sequentially in sympathy with the upper parts, as in the canon in the unison; only here greater freedom is the result, since the canon is not in the unison, and the sequential repetitions therefore do not produce the same chords. But whatever freedom Bach takes with his intermediate chords the cadences always reproduce the original scheme faithfully.

composer seems to have escaped notice. Yet I have an old volume containing the original edition (with list of subscribers) of six amiably ineffective Clavier Sonatas, and a still more amiable and ineffective set of twenty-four *Veränderungen für Clavichord oder Fortepiano auf das englische Volkslied*: *God Save the King*. To any one who knows the 'Goldberg' Variations, these variations of Forkel are a source of pure and innocent joy. To prepare himself for writing the first biography of Bach, Forkel must needs write a few more 'Goldberg' Variations, *auf das englische Volkslied*. He does not attempt canons, for he is no contrapuntist, nor does he write for two keyboards, as his instrument did not possess them, but he faithfully reproduces the outward semblance of the other salient points in Bach's work, regardless of the fact that *das englische Volkslied* is far too short for variations in such strongly individualized forms. Bach makes his tenth variation a complete four-part fughetta, so Forkel does likewise with his fourteenth. At least it sounds vaguely like something in a fugato style and in an indeterminate number of parts (generally two, where extra notes are not put in to fill up the harmony), and in order to strengthen the reader's faith Forkel writes 'Fugetta' (so spelt) above it. Later on in the work he gives still more touching testimony to his admiration of the 'Goldberg' Variations, not without signs of talent, though his innocence is marvellous, even as the innocence of a Babu journalist. However, it is well that Bach's first biographer should have shown that in 1791, eleven years before his Bach biography, he knew and loved the 'Goldberg' Variations; perhaps better than many subsequent critics have done.

To return to Bach, the eleventh variation is once more, as we have learnt to expect, a brilliant duet. Its first idea, imitations for the two hands, with that incessant crossing that is so natural with two keyboards—

Ex. 27

alternates with a new pair of themes in the next four-bar phrase:

Ex. 28

The substitution of C♯ for C in the sixth step of the Base is very telling, and in no way impairs the clearness and simplicity with which the harmonic scheme is presented in these duet-variations. As in all the duets, the material changes and develops as the variation proceeds.

The twelfth variation is the canon in the fourth. Now at this interval there seems at first sight but little possibility of producing such characteristic effects as Bach has produced in the former canons. The fourth and fifth are intervals in which the answer differs but little from the subject in arrangement of tones and semitones and the resulting expression; while at such distances the parts will have no natural tendency to cross. On the other hand, the fourth and fifth, as intervals for a canon, produce one effect that has considerable harmonic value, since they cause the tonic to be answered by the dominant, and vice versa, thus bringing the cardinal points of the key into effective antithesis.

Bach is determined that his canons in the fourth and fifth shall be as vitally and characteristically canonic as the earlier ones; therefore the canon in the fourth begins with phrases that throw the notes of tonic and dominant into strong relief both at their beginnings and ends, so that the answer puts corresponding weight on dominant and tonic. And in order that his canon may not lack other characteristics, he makes it by inversion; where the subject rises the answer descends, and vice versa. Further, he makes the inversion absolutely clear to the ear, first by con-structing his subject out of figures that move in long streams of scale steadily up and down, and secondly by alternating these scales with long notes and rests, through which the answer, moving gracefully with a droll persistence in the opposite direc-tion, cannot fail to be easily heard (see p. 51).

As the canonic parts move in opposite directions, the character-istic antithesis between tonic and dominant (marked T and D in the quotation) is the more prominent, since these are the only notes in the two parts which show a definite harmonic relation-ship to each other. Where the whole organization of the canonic parts is so transparent, and the expression so full of delicate humour,[1] there is no need for special treatment of the harmonic scheme, and the Base in this variation is hardly more disguised than in the original theme. In the second half the order of canon is changed; the lower part leading with (a) inverted on the dominant, answered, of course, by the upper part a fourth higher with (a) direct on the tonic.

Though this canon can hardly be said, in view of its open tex-

---

[1] E.g., the odd displacement of rhythm in the fifth and sixth bars, a touch that would surely reveal the *effect* (though not the *name*) of canonic structure even to a listener who had never heard contrapuntal music before.

ture, to have a complex effect, it certainly has more than the usual expression of whimsical obstinacy. So Bach continues on the lines he has so far established, and follows it by something luxuriously clear and steady, after which another brilliant two-part instrumental display completes and diverts the reaction. This time, however, the reaction from the canon takes a fresh form. The thirteenth variation is clear, steady, and luxurious, but not with the polyphony of the fourth and tenth variations, nor with the dance-rhythm and simple tunefulness of the seventh.

Ex. 29

It takes us, for the first time in the work, to the very home of Bach's intensely human art. So far we have had grace, brilliance, wit, dignity, and a certain tender solemnity here and there (e.g. Var. 9); but now Bach pours forth a stream of his inexhaustible florid melody—melody whose ornamentation is totally different from the delicate but undoubtedly posing manner of the Aria. Put the Aria and the thirteenth variation side by side, and a glance at the printed page will show the difference between the shakes and mordents of the former, indicated as they are by signs, and the fully-written and highly-individualized arabesques of the latter. It is strange to think that within living memory this wonderful florid style was supposed to be 'quaint rococo'! Bach is never more profoundly a modern, a writer for all time, never more intimately human and directly expressive than when he gives us his most florid melody.

This thirteenth variation is a trio, but, unlike the second variation and canons, it is the two lower parts that are kept together while the upper part stands alone. The immense stream of florid melody contains at least four distinct ideas arranged so as to make the elaborate details of rhythm crowd closer and closer from the opening—

Ex.30 Solo melody

through syncopation—

Ex.31

to the unbroken demisemiquavers:

Ex.32

that subside into the beautiful drooping cadence-figure:

Ex.33

Meanwhile the twin lower parts (which adhere very closely to the Base) swing on in their firm, characteristic rhythm, supporting and throwing into relief the melody which, if they were to cease, would be poured away like water from a broken vessel. In this variation as in its better-known but not more lovely archetype, the andante of the 'Italian' Concerto, we find a revelation of the meaning and truth of Chopin's dictum on tempo rubato; that the right hand plays in a free declamatory style, while the left preserves the normal rhythm as a guide.

The fourteenth variation (being the second after a canon) is, as usual, a brilliant duet. But now that the range of contrast has begun to increase, the element of instrumental display becomes still more prominent, and this variation surprises us with far more brilliance than any we have yet heard.

The four ideas that appear in the first half—

are reproduced in the same order in the second half, but almost all by inversion.

And now, as soon as this exhilarating variation is over, we come to the first great dramatic stroke in the course of the tremendous design. The fifteenth variation is the half-way house; let us take breath and look back on what we have seen so far. The first two variations were finely devised to open our minds for the reception of larger and more brilliant things than the light-hearted and much-adorned Aria suggested. Then came the exceptionally complex and subtle canon in the unison, throwing into the strongest light the characteristics of the contrapuntal devices that were to form so prominent a feature throughout the work. From this point onwards we became aware of the happy arrangement of the variations in a regular rotation of canon, a clear-cut and highly rhythmic variation, and a brilliant running duet. Thanks to this grouping, and to the increase of character in the clear-cut variations, and of brilliance in the duets, we had learnt, when we reached the splendid little fughetta, that this was a work of surprising adroitness and inexhaustible variety. With the thirteenth variation we learn something more: the design suddenly 'broadens and deepens'. The variety is not merely confined to changes of form, style, and rhythm; indeed, for the first time in the work, Bach dispenses with radical changes of rhythm, and writes three variations together in 3/4 time; a fact which, in spite of their contrasts in speed, internal rhythm, and expression, greatly strengthens our feeling that the work is now entering a stage at which the lines of its design become vastly larger. As in the thirteenth variation Bach shows a new depth of feeling, so, in accordance with the laws of human nature and art, he shows in the fourteenth a corresponding increase in fullness of high spirits. And after that, the reaction is tremendous. Again we learn something new of the work. It is not merely a work of great beauty of feeling: it is one that tells of bitter experience. The fifteenth variation is, of course, the canon in the fifth; and, like that in the fourth, it is by inversion. All the measures Bach took to make the inverse canon in the fourth intelligible as such, he takes here. There is the same clear antithesis between tonic in the subject, and dominant in the answer, and vice versa; and the same care to bring out the effect of inverse motion, by making the subject take long upward and downward journeys instead of hovering without clearly marked direction. And there is the same use of long notes as transparent spaces through which the answer may be heard.

But there is none of the droll capriciousness that we saw in the canon in the fourth here. Bach has made a more radical change than any merely rhythmic one. He has put this fifteenth variation in the minor mode, which not only affects all the harmonies of the scheme, but completely alters some of the keys, and of course cannot fail to cast a shade of melancholy over the whole—unless the composer chose to counteract it by other rhythmic and melodic characteristics. This, however, Bach does not do; he writes some of his saddest and bitterest music here. The bass is of course mainly occupied in translating the Base of the theme, very closely at first, but with some freedom in the second half. Yet it is no less expressive than the upper parts, whose material (especially figure (a)) it frequently shares. Note its powerful and poignant expression in the third bar, where it so boldly alternates the two possible translations of the third step in the Base (E♮ and E♭):

Ex. 38

In the second half the key of E minor is translated by that of E flat major, as E minor is not naturally related to G minor. In bars 21 to 24 the canonic parts come to close quarters in a complex way that may perhaps be easier to follow when we see them on separate staves. They only bring out the characteristic canonic effect more strikingly and freshly by their momentary coincidence:

Ex. 39

Then the lower canonic part crosses the bass, and as both are very expressive it is well to disentangle them also:

Ex. 40

The last four bars bring this variation, and the first half of the great work, to a very impressive close.

If such directions had been appreciated at the time, Bach might have headed his next variation *Neue Kraft fühlend*, as Beethoven heads the vigorous alternative theme in the *Heiliger Dankgesang eines Genesenen* in his A minor Quartet. Bach's sixteenth variation bursts forth, after the sombre tones of the fifteenth, with a 'feeling of renewed strength', not unworthy to be regarded as a foreshadowing of that so wonderfully expressed by Beethoven in his 'pious thanksgiving of one restored to health'.

This variation is one of the most audacious experiments Bach ever made, and the audacity is, as usual, forgotten in the perfect maturity of the result. All the variations are in forms that may be found elsewhere in suites, preludes, and other instrumental works.[1] But in this sixteenth variation Bach gives us a bolder reproduction of large independent art-forms than we should have thought conceivable within the limits of his theme. He actually works out its two halves as separate movements in contrasted tempi, the whole forming a classical 'French Overture'. Thus the new chapter in the great work is ushered in with all the pomp and circumstance with which Handel would open an oratorio or opera.

The first half of the variation is the stately introductory movement. It has all the usual features of the style—dotted notes, short runs, and a full and emphatic manner:

Ex. 41

Base and harmonies are clearly reproduced, though the slow tempo and long bars cause some natural interpolations to enter between the later steps.

[1] The duets may be matched (on a larger scale) in the *Wohltemperirtes Clavier* by such preludes as the G major and B flat major of the second book, very slightly disguised by an occasional harmonic filling-out. The trios of the canonic type, where the upper parts are treated as twins over an independent bass, may be found (without the restrictions of canon) in the E major Prelude of the second book, the Sarabande of the G major Partita, all the slow movements of the organ sonatas, or, to quote once more the great canonic example, the Andante of the A major Violin Sonata. The four-part variations (except the fughetta) are of precisely the same texture as the A minor Fantasia, the C major and F major Preludes in the second book of the *Wohltemperirtes Clavier*, and the Adagios near the beginning of the C minor and F sharp minor Toccatas. The seventh variation is on the same lines as the Gigues of the C minor French Suite and the French Overture; and lastly the trios of the form in which a florid melody stands out from the background of a two-part bass, are exactly like the famous Andante of the 'Italian' Concerto and the G minor Prelude (and also, to some extent, the E major) in the first book of the *Wohltemperirtes Clavier*.

The second half of the variation is the quick movement in a fugued style. Its first chord overlaps with the last of the preceding movement, according to the invariable usage in French Overtures, thus producing the one solitary liberty Bach takes with his rhythmic framework in the whole work. It is usual and desirable that the quick movement should be the principal part of the overture, both as to length and material; but Bach is here limited by his theme, in which the second part is of exactly the same length as the first. Moreover, the very fact that this overture form must be expressed on so small a scale makes it desirable that the contrast between the slow introduction and the quick principal movement should be more clearly marked than usual; so that Bach chooses 3/8 time for his second part to bring out this contrast by means of very short bars. Thus everything conspires to make the second part dwindle to insignificance by the side of the first; but here Bach's usual tact easily remedies the situation. In the first place he makes two bars of his 3/8 movement stand for one of the theme (the only case in the whole work where the correspondence is not either bar for bar or half-bar for bar)—shown by the numbers given below the following quotation, as compared with the Base:

Ex.42

In the second place, he treats the harmonies with considerable freedom towards the end, so as to obliterate the extreme regularity of the theme (which distributes its cadences exactly once in every four bars), and give the impression of a freely flowing movement. And, in the third place, the player can help to give the second part due emphasis by repeating it and not repeating the first. Lastly, it is, after all, not Bach's object to give the impression of a fully developed overture on a large scale at the expense of the proportions of what is, after all, only one of thirty variations. His intention is that after the fifteenth variation has closed the first half of his work with a chapter of sadness and gloom the sixteenth variation should usher in the second with promise of a larger and fuller life than anything the listener has yet learned to expect from it. For this purpose the audacious indication of the main facts of the two-movement overture form is more effective than a complete working out. The whole thing is most brilliant and telling, from the first chord (which startles us as being the first solid block of harmony that we have yet heard—standing out thus prominently in the middle of a work of which hitherto every note has been the result of contrapuntal part-writing) to the last, which Bach carefully writes as a long note to be held down for its full value.[1]

As we now expect of the second variation after a canon, the seventeenth variation is a brilliant duet. It is entirely founded on its initial pair of themes (of which (b) is much developed by inversion)—

Ex.43

and takes more advantage of the possibilities of two keyboards than any we have yet heard.

The eighteenth variation is the canon in the sixth. Now that the intervals of canon have become so wide that the parts do not readily cross, and the device of inversion has been twice used in slow variations with long bars, Bach changes his methods of canonic writing altogether. Hitherto the themes of his canons have been like any other kind of melody, conspicuously free from those turns of phrase and rhythm that the experience alike of listeners and composers recognizes as specially adapted for academic contrapuntal development. Bach, addressing his canons to the ear, has made his leading melodies such as can be identified when the answering part reproduces them. The turns and rhythms of ordinary counterpoint would not have been distinctive enough for such a purpose. But now he has a use for them. The point is an important one, and the reader will perhaps pardon a digression in illustration of it.

There is a dangerous common fallacy that what is technically conventional is always artistically lifeless. In every art and every faculty there is a certain technical sense of the word 'conventional', which implies no adverse criticism and is in no sense inconsistent with originality. Certain turns of phrase and certain

---

[1] Incredible as it may seem, Forkel has made one of his variations an overture too! The result is so touching (especially with so short and familiar a theme) that I cannot refrain from quoting it in an Appendix.

devices carry with them obvious signs of a capacity for certain kinds of development. These turns and devices are therefore very soon brought into constant use, until a time comes when they have grown to be so familiar that, as with many simple metaphors and catch-words in language, much of their true meaning is lost through their being used in an unintelligent and apathetic manner. They are then said to be 'conventional', and just because it is easy to see the absurdity of a meaningless use of them, there arises a considerable danger of our failing to understand them when great men use them with the full force of their true original meaning, deepened by a new context and new functions. Nothing is more characteristic than Bach's use of the conventional turns of phrase that are typical of pure counterpoint. They became conventional types just because their capacity for easy contrapuntal treatment was almost self-evident alike to ear and eye. Therefore it is easy contrapuntal treatment that Bach gives them; his counterpoint is never so transparent and simple as when his subjects and rhythms are most nearly those of an exercise in those 'Five Species of Counterpoint' in which we train the student of composition as scholars are trained to write Latin and Greek verses. On the other hand, Bach always uses these formulas to convey something they never conveyed before; and if they never conveyed it before that must have been because it was not a thing that they were obviously capable of conveying. That is to say, their very conventionality is the essence of their originality in Bach's hands; he uses them in a way that shows his deep understanding of their real meaning as known in former times, while he reveals capacities in them that were hitherto unknown. The great D minor Organ Fugue (so-called 'Doric') is an excellent instance on the largest scale; the themes and style are in every detail 'conventional contrapuntal', and the counterpoint is extremely clear and simple, just as it would have been in the hands of the first composers who used themes of such a type. But the most thoroughly conventional phrase of all is, throughout the work, put into positions where its contrapuntal treatment, otherwise conventional enough, gives rise to harmonies of unheard-of boldness and strength. The phrase dates from an age in which discords were used with extreme caution, and the positions into which Bach puts it were, before his time, rejected as manifestly wrong and inconceivable. A composer with the ordinary modern views as to originality would, had he lived in Bach's day, have rejected the phrase itself, with all the conventional developments that it obviously suggested; but Bach saw that there were other developments that it did not so obviously suggest; and hence arose a gigantic work.

This may seem a wide digression from our 'Goldberg' Variations; but it helps us to realize that Bach's originality is not altogether on the lines laid down by popular criticism, and that his methods are far removed alike from those of mere scholasticism and anti-academic irritability. Any less great composer would most assuredly have made all these nine canons out of obviously contrapuntal subject-matter, whereas Bach reserves his piece of pure 'fourth and fifth species of counterpoint' to a later part of the work, where it enters as something entirely new and unheard-of. It is one of the smoothest and clearest of all the variations; and it is easy for the ear to recognize it as a canon in the sixth, because the answer follows the subject so closely that almost every note in the one overlaps with the corresponding note in the other, so that the two parts are actually heard as moving in sixths all but simultaneously from beginning to end.

Ex. 44   Answer   Subject   &c.

The smooth chain of suspensions and the typical 'fifth species' rhythms sound strangely fresh and original as used here to express a structure of more than usual symmetry of form, for the conventional turns and rhythms of 'pure counterpoint' suggest anything rather than clear-cut designs such as characterize the forms of the suite or the modern sonata. Bach, however, almost always works out these conventional figures into unusually clear formal designs, as here, where the last eight bars of the second half are note for note those of the last eight of the first half transposed to the tonic, a touch of formality that has never occurred before in the work. Another most effective vitalizing feature is that while much of the bass is constructed so as to give the harmonies of the theme without reproducing the actual notes of its Base, the latter may often be quite clearly identified for as much as four bars together in the canonic parts, thus giving them yet another interest that one would never expect from their external style. It is interesting to see on such a small scale the qualities which make the A minor Fantasia one of Bach's most stirring compositions. In later music, as for instance the finale of Mozart's 'Jupiter' Symphony, we may sometimes see the same principles 'writ large', so large that the mind does not always find it easy to take them in.

The canon in the sixth has been so clear and its bars so short that Bach follows it with another short-bar variation with something of the same vitalized-conventional character; this being the first time that two short-bar variations have come together. This nineteenth variation is a trio of a new type, in which a flowing semiquaver figure is passed from part to part, penetrating easily through its transparent and more sustained accompaniments:

Ex.45

The twentieth variation, being the second after a canon, is, of course, a brilliant duet, the most brilliant we have yet heard. It contrasts very effectively with the last three variations in the unusual quantity and variety of its figures. (Here we may as well note that Bach has shown his usual wisdom in giving those three variations a single idea apiece, as a contrast and relief after his strange *tour de force* in making the sixteenth variation consist of two independent movements.)

There are no less than three pairs of themes and about eight distinct figures, all of which are treated by inversion as well as in direct form, even in the first half of the variation. And in the second half a new and most effective idea appears towards the end, greatly increasing the excitement and bustle of the whole movement.

It will suffice to quote only the first two pairs of ideas—

Ex. 46

and—

Ex.47

(both parts promptly inverted).

The other ideas are reproduced very symmetrically in the second part; room being found for the new one, alluded to above, by crowding those just quoted into a smaller space.

As the work proceeds, important events in the design happen more frequently. The first change to the minor mode happened half-way through the work, at the fifteenth variation. Only six variations later we come to the second. Once more we plunge from the height of energy and brilliance into a dark and melancholy reaction. But there is less bitterness here, and more tenderness. It is as if the larger experience and fuller joy of life had tempered this second reaction with a new sympathy, preparing the mind for yet greater joys and that wonderful sense of *lachrymae rerum* which (in the twenty-fifth variation) is given more moving voice than ever came from any other artist save Beethoven.

The canon in the seventh is very easily followed as such; the distance between the parts preventing them from crossing, and the answer being in the upper part. Moreover, the answer enters somewhat closely after the subject, with the result that when in the second half Bach has to make changes of key, the characteristic effect of the answer wresting the phrases of the subject into the harmonies of the key a minor seventh higher (or tone lower) is very clearly felt.

The following quotation will show how Bach translates into chromatic steps the four downward diatonic steps with which his Base began. Half-bars correspond to the bars of the original theme:

Ex. 48

The continuation I have quoted in the Introduction (p. 30), as an example of those intentional strange touches of harmony with which Bach enhances alike the expression and the clearness of texture in his canons. The Base and harmonies of the original theme are translated more closely than at first sight appears. In the second half matters are somewhat disguised by the fact that E minor must be translated by E flat, but the startling harmonies that occur during the process are not really unfaithful to the original, while at the same time they make the relation between the canonic parts more obvious to the ear. The last bar of the variation is very subtle and effective. Note how ingeniously the beautiful flat supertonic (A flat) is introduced as an appogiatura in the subject, so as to produce in the answer the tonic G as its last note:

Ex. 49

In the twenty-second variation Bach continues the plan (which he has never really abandoned) of following the canons by something clear-cut, solid, and luxurious. Here the contrast is, of course, strengthened by the return to the major mode. The variation is of the third type, four-part contrapuntal treatment of a simple figure, such as we had in the fourth variation. Here the figure is of the same conventional 'fifth species' type as that of the canon in the sixth, but it is treated in a different way, being piled into fully harmonized rising sequences that attain a certain architectural grandeur, which seems once more to enlarge the range of the work as did the overture, though, of course, the feeling is not so strong here. The Base is here as simple as in the theme:

After this we have, of course, another brilliant duet; but a more madcap frolic than even Bach ever wrote in any other instrumental work. It has been a much discussed point whether Bach had a sense of humour, and as long as we try to settle the matter by quoting phrases here and there which may sound humorous if played quickly, but are no less certainly solemn in a slow tempo, we shall not be much the wiser. But we can have no doubts in a case like the twenty-third 'Goldberg' Variation, which is merely dull and unintelligible in a slow tempo, but is one sparkling tissue of excellent fooling, from the first phrase, with its close canon and its displaced spasmodic little runs in the fourth bar (see over)—

Ex. 51

through the second principal idea, with its mordents, **its absurd rhythm**, and its obstinate contrary motion—

Ex 52

to the last six bars, in which (for the first time in the work, since the chords in the overture) vocal part-writing is cast to the winds, and the two hands (and keyboards) divide a passage in thirds, as follows—

Ex 53

the resulting sense being, of course—

Ex. 54

but with a curious variegated tone unattainable by ordinary methods.

It is as impossible to dispute the playful humour of such a variation as to dispute that of the aria of Midas in *Der Streit zwischen Phoebus und Pan*, where, *before* he is punished by having his ears turned into those of an ass, the violins greet his reference to 'the judgement of my ears' with a delightfully musical 'hee-haw':

Ex. 55

It is true that Bach seldom has occasion for such direct manifestations of a jocular spirit; and we cannot expect even these things to appeal to those modern wits who look for humour nowhere except in things 'gruff and grim', and accordingly find none in earlier music than Beethoven, and little but gruffness and grimness there. It must also undoubtedly be conceded that Bach, like Homer and most of the ancient classics, is always (in a certain sense) literal. With him a joke is always a joke, and play is essentially play, undertaken with the same singleness of mind as the most serious matters. But this, though it may debar him from the infinite subtleties and conflicts of feeling which characterize more modern art, in no way affects the question whether he possesses a true sense of humour. That is a matter of temperament and sympathy, not of resource. If the art-language is thoroughly literal, as was classical Greek, then all the natural artistic devices will be literal too, and most attempts at more ironical forms of expression will lack one of the first conditions of true humour—spontaneity. It is only in a later and more complex art-world that the normal means of expression are sufficiently figurative for an artist to express himself spontaneously by combining contrasted feelings in a manner more complex and less capable of analysis than that of earlier classics. We must not expect to find in Bach that humour which consists in exciting strong incompatible emotions at the same moment. In art of such simplicity of principle and resource, this would be no humour, but mere paradox, utterly lacking in spontaneity and truth. It is enough for us, indeed it *is* the more modern humour translated into the simpler terms of earlier art, that Bach can in the same work write an extravaganza like the twenty-third variation, and in the twenty-fifth touch some of the profoundest chords of sympathy and sorrow that art possesses. An artist without humour can sometimes produce great works, but he would be terrified at the idea of bringing playful passages into them; and,

F

on the other hand, he would certainly make painful mistakes which Bach never made—the unintentionally ridiculous effects. It is not Bach but Handel who in a solemn oratorio portrays the plague of frogs by a stately aria accompanied with hopping figures on the violins.

After the twenty-third variation comes the canon in the octave, a splendidly dignified movement with a broad swinging rhythm that seems well fitted to bring the third great chapter of the work to a climax:

Ex. 56

The answer is two entire bars later than the subject, and at such a wide interval of pitch that the canon is more transparent than any we have hitherto had, especially as the interval of an octave makes the answer and subject identical in harmonic meaning. Bach takes advantage of these facts to change his canon once in every eight bars. Thus in the ninth bar the lower part breaks off its imitation and begins leading with a new canon, imitated (at the same distance as before) by the upper part in the higher octave:

Ex. 57   (b)

The figure marked (*b*) in Ex. 57 is used to conclude each eight-bar phrase throughout the variation. In the second half the lower part leads the canon for eight bars (or, rather, six as it rests while the answer is finishing two bars later), after which the upper part resumes leadership:

Ex. 58

And now we come to the greatest chapter in the whole work, the wonderful song of sorrow that reveals to us the full human sympathy and beauty of Bach's mind, and by its profound and tender pathos prepares us to triumph in that final outburst of highest joy with which the work comes to its climax.

The twenty-fifth variation is a trio of the same type as the thirteenth, a florid melody on a clearly rhythmic two-part bass. In Ex. 8 I have already quoted the device of filling out the Base with intermediate chromatic steps, and we have seen another incidental instance of it at the beginning of the canon in the seventh. But here in the twenty-fifth variation it becomes a fixed principle, and leads to very astonishing results in harmony and expression. The tempo is very slow and the bars very long, so that in a single bar a phrase of considerably developed organization is expressed:

Ex. 59

Now let the bass move downward, like the Base of the theme, with the steps chromatically filled out, and on this construct a sequential repetition of the whole phrase, melody and all, a tone lower:

Ex. 60

The result is a most extraordinary and telling transition through F minor, of all keys the one most contrary to the tonic.

Yet the Base is preserved absolutely faithfully here and throughout the variation; indeed, it can be followed in one or the other
of the two lower parts note for note more easily and completely
than almost anywhere else in the whole work. In the second half
E minor must (as is inevitable in a minor variation) be translated
by E flat; but Bach takes advantage of the firm and highly organized form of his melody, and the great clearness with which the
steps of his Base are preserved, and he makes the key E flat
minor. Four entire bars (and that in this very slow tempo),
corresponding to bars 25–8, are in this distant key; a fact that
we should refuse to believe even of Bach, if we had not the passage before us to prove and justify it. The transition from E flat
minor through its major chord to C minor, and the resumption
in that key of the initial subject with its consequent descent
through B flat minor (another incredibly distant key), all founded
on the clearest possible steps in the bass—these things further
intensify the thrill of this wonderful movement, which culminates in an immensely broad descending sequence, no less than
six steps long, as the melody gathers its passionate rhythms
together in a single steady flow, while the bass, no less expressive
throughout the variation, rises to meet it, and ends above it:

Ex. 61

Thus the last great emotional outburst in the work closes.
Three times the artist's grand scheme has carried us through
passages of profound sadness: the first time the tones have been
bitter and indignant; the second time there has been a note of
tenderness; but now the artist has made the greatest sadness of
all the means of expressing the loveliest and most touching traits
in a great man's character.

The last chapter of the work begins, as we should expect,
brilliantly; still fulfilling the spirit of Bach's plan of making the
second variation after each canon a brilliant duet. But this time
it is the spirit and not the letter that is fulfilled.

The twenty-sixth variation is not a duet, but a new kind of
trio, in which one part is a running stream, while the other two
move together in a steady sarabande rhythm with a melody on
their surface:

Ex. 62

The runs, beginning below the sarabande parts, soon pass above
them. After the first eight bars the running part is assigned to
the left hand as bass, the right hand taking up the sarabande
material. In the second half the running figure is inverted, and
towards the end of the variation both treble and bass are seized
by the torrent, bringing the movement to a brilliant climax.

Before the final outburst, Bach gives a short breathing space
in the shape of his last canon, that in the ninth:

Ex. 63

It is playful, graceful, and easier to follow as a canon than any of
the former, since it differs from them in having no third free part
below the two engaged in the canon. Here the canonic parts
stand alone, and the frequent staccato notes (e.g., second bar)
and strongly marked rhythms make the structure extremely
transparent. As an offset to this, now that there is no non-canonic
element present, Bach returns to his practice in the earlier canons,
of treating the harmonies with some freedom; especially in
obliterating the intermediate cadences of the theme (about bars
8 and 24). In the second half the canon changes, the upper part
leading with a free inversion of the initial subject:

Ex. 64

After this playful, but comparatively quiet little movement, the great triumphal spectacle begins. Strict part-writing is partly abandoned, and we plunge into four pages of purely instrumental writing of the most brilliant character. The look of the printed pages suggests Thalberg or even Liszt, rather than a contra-puntist of the eighteenth century. Certainly the 'false trills', with which the twenty-eighth variation begins—

Ex. 65 (a)
(b)

are more suggestive of the nineteenth century than Scarlatti's most extravagant freaks of harpsichord-writing. Like the earlier strict duets this twenty-eighth variation has a second idea—

Ex. 66 (c)
(c) inverse   &c.

of which the lower (inverse) part is in the second half combined with an inversion of (b) (Ex. 53).

The grouping of materials is not at all symmetrical, and alternations are rapid and capricious. Towards the end, a chro-matic scale in quavers adds much to the excitement.

One variation is not enough to work up to the full triumphant climax, so Bach continues in the twenty-ninth with further developments of instrumental brilliance. This is the only case in the whole work where he has put together two variations of the same type, and in the same tempo and rhythm. (The eleventh, twelfth, and thirteenth variations were, as we observed in discussing them, all in 3/4 time, but in very different tempi, let us say—moderato, andante sostenuto, and allegro. But the present pair of variations are in almost exactly the same tempo, the second, perhaps, a shade faster. Elsewhere throughout the work a moment's inspection will show that each variation has a different time-signature from that of its neighbours.)

It is unnecessary to discuss the extremely brilliant twenty-ninth variation further than by quoting its two principal ideas—

Ex. 67

and—

Ex. 68

and observing how, as usual, fresh incidents arise in its latter portion, enhancing the excitement and variety already produced by the extreme brilliance and unsymmetrical alternations of its principal material.[1]

And now how is the great work to be brought to a worthy conclusion? There are no possibilities in Bach's art for the organization of a large free coda, such as a modern composer would feel obliged to provide for a work of even a quarter of these dimensions. And Bach's theme is not, like that of his great Organ Passacaglia, a short well-marked piece of melody which may be turned into the subject of a fugue. Until one has actually experienced the work as a whole, it seems incredible that the end to which Bach brings it should produce a really satisfactory and final effect; yet no sooner has one heard it than one is convinced that Bach's rounding-off is alone that which has no redundancy and leaves nothing unexpressed. Brilliance the work has, as no earlier work ever suggested; but brilliance is not its keynote. Its keynote is human interest and happiness, and with human happiness and peace it ends. After his triumphs the hero returns to his home, and a very simple home it is too, breathing a royal atmosphere of good feeling and happiness. Here they sit round

[1] Forkel has epitomized these two variations (*plus* scraps of the twentieth) in the most amusing way in his set. I give examples in the Appendix.

the hearth and sing folk-songs with infinite spirit and zest. The thirtieth variation is a 'Quodlibet'; that is, a contrapuntal hotch-potch of popular tunes. In Bach's time, when the tunes were widely known, the result must have been very amusing. To us there remains the pure, artistic exhilaration caused by the obviously popular style of the subjects and the immense swing of their setting, points which are, after all, the same as those which really told in Bach's own day.

Two of Bach's tunes have been traced and their original words found. One of them is—

Ex.69

† Ich   bin   so   lang bei   dir   nicht   g'west

† i.e., *Gewesen.* 'It is so long since I have been at your house.'

and the other is—

Ex.70

‡Kraut und   Rü - ben   ha-ben mich ver   trie - ben,

‡ 'Cabbage and turnips have driven me away. If my mother'd cooked some meat, I might have stopped longer.'

with its second part (which Bach combines in double counter-point with the first):

Ex.71

Hätt' mein' Mut-ter Fleisch geko-cht,   So   wär   ich läng-er   g'blie - ben

With these and some other phrases that have not been identified, Bach constructs on his Base (very faithfully reproduced) an elaborate and stirring little chorus, making a four-part variation of the third type, as in Variations 4, 10, and 22. Having thus crowned his grand design by taking us, with an irresistible friendliness, into his very home, Bach rounds it off by showing us the one thing we have forgotten, though without it the work could never have existed. At least, we have forgotten its outward surface, though its Base and harmonies have guided every step in the work. The Aria returns in its original shape, with a strangely new and yet familiar effect. Its numberless trills and graces no longer seem curious and posing, and its harmonies are now revealed as what they really are, the support of the whole mighty design, not merely the bass of a delicately-ornamented sarabande. As the Aria gathers up its rhythms into the broad

passage of steady semiquavers with which it ends, we realize that
beneath its slight exterior the great qualities of the variations lie
concealed, but living and awake; and in the moment that we
realize this the work is over.

APPENDIX

Forkel's Overture

Forkel's epitomes of Bach's twentieth, twenty-eighth, and twenth-ninth variations:

Ex.73 First part of Var. 22

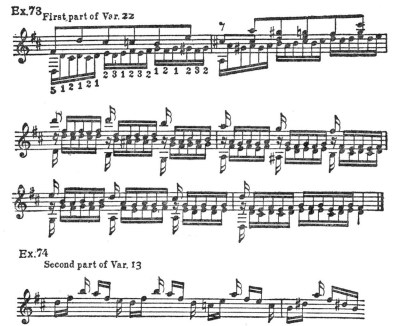

Ex. 74
Second part of Var. 13

It is strange to speculate on the bewilderment such passages would cause us, supposing (as might easily have happened considering what great works of Bach have been completely lost[1]) that the 'Goldberg' Variations had, like most of his works, not been published in his lifetime and that the manuscripts had been lost since Forkel saw them. What a mystery Forkel's Overture would be then! How utterly impossible to guess his motive for such an absurd experiment! And, strangest of all, the subsequent history of variation-writing would have hardly been affected, for though Beethoven knew the 'Goldberg' Variations, and to some extent worked under their influence when he wrote his great set of thirty-three, yet his methods are so different and so vastly

[1] e.g., the *Passion* according to St. Mark, known to be a mature work on a larger scale than that according to St. John.

more complex that there is little doubt that he would eventually have arrived at the same result, whether he knew Bach's great set or not. Forkel's work would have remained an unfathomable (but ridiculous and isolated) mystery for all time if its inspiring source had been lost.

4. A LISTENER'S GUIDE TO 'DIE KUNST DER FUGE'
(1936)

BACH'S *Kunst der Fuge* is a series of fugues demonstrating all the principal types and devices of fugue, from the simplest to the most complex. All the fugues have the same theme, though some begin with other themes which afterwards combine with it. In order to display the texture of the work, Bach wrote it in open score, showing thereby that it is written, like most of his fugues, for a definite number of voices which do not become confused. This conceals the almost equally important fact that, with two exceptions, these fugues are keyboard music as strictly practical as those in *Das Wohltemperirte Clavier*. Some modern editors have denied this, but it is not a matter of opinion at all; he who denies it merely shows that he has never been taught to play from score, an art which ought to be, as it was in Bach's time, one of the elementary items in a musical education. No passage in *Die Kunst der Fuge* is quite as difficult as the E flat Prelude in the first book of *Das Wohltemperirte Clavier*. The end of the unfinished fugue, where four subjects are combined and inverted, would necessarily have been the most difficult passage in the whole work; and in my conjectural execution of it I have found no difficulty in keeping to the strict rules of keyboard-writing for two hands.

With the exception of the last side, on which I recorded my conjectural finish on the pianoforte, the set of gramophone records to accompany which this essay was written, presents *Die Kunst der Fuge* through the medium of a string quartet, and thus enables the listener to hear the part-writing in perfect clarity. Such an opportunity is rare, and Mozart, whose own part-playing on the pianoforte left nothing to be desired, actually took the trouble to write out several four-part fugues of *Das Wohltemperirte Clavier* for string quartet in order to enjoy the effect. It is by no means a matter of course that keyboard fugues will stand the test. An extra note, amplifying a chord here and there, does not matter: Bach allows himself one, two, or even three extra parts in the last bars of Nos. V, VI, VII, and XI of *Die Kunst der Fuge*. But the keyboard fugues of Mendelssohn simply cannot be put into score at all; they sound smooth and classical, but the parts have no integrity; one chord has **four**

notes and the next has three, and a fifth may appear from nowhere. There are no threads that quartet-players could follow.
Handel's fugues are nearly as loose, but not so confused; he
will thicken his bass with octaves and chords, and on the other
hand, his middle part or parts will seldom be likely to put in
more than a perfunctory appearance after the opening. You may
perhaps be surprised to hear that Beethoven and Schumann are
as scrupulous as Bach in maintaining real part-writing in their
fugues. Beethoven need hardly have apologized for his *alcune
licenze* in the enormous three-part fugue in the Sonata, op. 106;
and Schumann not only put much thoughtful part-writing into
his *Six Fugues on the Name of Bach*, but actually incorporated in
the finale of his *Impromptus*, op. 5, a very amusing and spirited
five-part fugue first written as a counterpoint exercise when he
was studying with Dehn.

Much enjoyment of music has been spoiled by false teaching
about the nature of part-writing. Psychologists tell us that it is
impossible to attend to more than two things at once. From this
it must follow that we cannot attend to all the four parts of these
fugues at once, and that it must be still more impossible to attend
to all the details of augmentation, diminution, stretto, inversion,
double, triple, and quadruple counterpoint through which Bach
develops his subject and countersubjects. But it ought never to
be supposed that any such attention is required of the listener.
Nothing prevents the listener from *hearing* all these things at once
and *attending* to one thing at a time. It is even doubtful whether
he need often, or ever, attend to two. If the complexity is artistic
it will make a single harmonious impression all the time, and the
attention will move with enjoyment from point to point according
as it is wisely directed.

The object of the present commentary is to direct the listener's
attention to what is immediately enjoyable, whether on a first
hearing or on intimate acquaintance. On a first hearing every
listener can enjoy the physical beauty of pure part-writing played
in perfect tune by a string quartet. This does not long remain an
object of attention; it soon passes into a state of musical comfort
which we do not wish to have disturbed. So long as that comfort lasts we are at leisure to attend to details, though the details
will hardly force themselves on us unless some disturbance of
the comfort arouses our attention. The masterly use of rough-
ness is, of course, one of the most important elements in art. In
music the word 'discord' has from quite early classical times
been as harmless a grammatical term as a 'transitive verb' or the
'accusative case'. The harmonic style of *Die Kunst der Fuge*
is often very bold. But at its boldest it is very smooth, notably
smoother than that of many earlier works of Bach, and it is

nowhere more smooth than where the combinations are most complex and most difficult for the composer to construct. Hence the listener must not expect that his attention will be roused by the ingenuity of this music at all. As the work becomes familiar, the listener will enjoy noticing many things which he would previously have supposed to be highly technical, and if he wishes to attain this enjoyment more speedily he will find in my *Companion to Bach's Art of Fugue* (Oxford University Press) a complete commentary on every aspect of the work which I have been able to follow. The same publishers have produced a score of the work embodying the results of my criticism of the text, with my supplementary completions; and they have also published pianoforte scores with my fingerings and indications of my views as to tempo and interpretation. Other editions, such as Peters, the Bach-Gesellschaft, Breitkopf and Härtel, have long been current and have been re-edited by other editors, mostly from quite different standpoints. Except for warning the listener that my own point of view is individual this is no occasion for controversy.

The listener will probably soon find his enjoyment much heightened by having the open score before him as he follows the records. The pianoforte score will serve the purpose up to a certain point: but the difficulty of following an open score written in the old clefs is greatly overrated at all times, and hardly exists at all in a case like this. You are not responsible for playing the notes, and strange clefs do not disguise the way in which the parts rise and fall. On the other hand the pianoforte reduction does often disguise passages in which the parts cross; and there are places in the *Wolhtemperirte Clavier* where even good scholars have accepted confused readings, though it is always possible to play the part-writing so that the ear can follow the correct sense.

CONTRAPUNCTUS I.—A simple figure on the following theme, which is the motto of the whole work.

Ex 1

Here your attention is claimed simply by the entries of this theme in one voice after another. The subtle details by which the 'answer' differs from the 'subject' are technicalities that need not concern the listener. In *Die Kunst der Fuge* Bach always preserves the whole subject, from first note to last. Accordingly, it is possible to distinguish between genuine entries and fragmentary allusions, such as often constitute the bulk of more loosely constructed fugues, like many of Handel's, where the subject is soon boiled to rags. Yet even in *Die Kunst der Fuge* the listener will find that, at all events after the first four fugues, it is as well to abandon the effort to count the entries of the subject. You obviously cannot tell whether the subject is complete until it has been completed: and in the higher orders of fugue the subject is only one of many elements that demand the attention, though it is the only thing that many pianoforte players have ever been taught to respect.

The passages during which no voice has the subject, or episodes, are in this first fugue purposely kept indefinite, though their length and rhetorical power increase as the work proceeds. The scale-figure marked (*a*) at the end of the subject can hardly fail to appear elsewhere in the counterpoint and episodes, such scales being an inevitable feature in most counterpoint, but on the whole Bach avoids all definite devices in this fugue except the entries of the subject. In one place the subject, in the treble, is answered in the bass before it has finished; and in two or three places its first three notes are anticipated or imitated by another voice. But, effective though this is, you should not take too much notice of it. The habit of hunting for such minutiae develops a vivid imagination for what is not there, but the fun is not worth the resulting total blindness to the plainest facts.

The portion of a fugue which comprises the first entries of all the voices is called the exposition. It may amuse the listener to verify the fact that, counting the four entries of the exposition, this fugue gives the theme ten times.

CONTRAPUNCTUS II merely shows that with the same simple organization, it is possible to write a fugue in a quite different mood. The scale-figure (*a*) is given a 'dotted' rhythm which struts through the whole fugue. In one place the first note of the subject is represented by upward steps in this rhythm.

Ex. 2

The first note of a fugue-subject is often liable to such variations, or to shortening, or to emerging from a longer note. Towards the end of this fugue the subject is syncopated.

CONTRAPUNCTUS III shows the emergence of organized counterpoint and of episodes that allude to one another. The theme is the inverted subject. Bach begins with what is really the answer, and when this is answered by the subject the first voice accompanies with a regular countersubject, as shown here:

Ex. 3

Countersubject

The countersubject accompanies, with one late exception, every entry of the subject, including several in which the subject is varied ornamentally as follows:

Ex. 4

(Such ornamental variations are not among the devices recognized by most text-books, for which Bach seems to have written in vain.)

The episodes arise from the chromatic figure marked (*b*), though there are also two short episodes derived from the scale-figure (*a*). It is now quite clear that the episodes are definite recurring ideas. The countersubject gives a chromatic character to the whole fugue, and in all probability Bach would have called this a chromatic fugue and classed it in a genus as such.

CONTRAPUNCTUS IV is also on the inverted subject. Its counter-point has figures which occasionally recur, but not regularly enough to constitute a countersubject. But its essential feature is the spacious and lively development of its episodes, which are among the most brilliant in *Die Kunst der Fuge*. They all arise from the scale-figure (*a*), running up and down, accompanied by a two-note figure of descending thirds. A grand rhetorical point is a series of entries in which part of the subject is raised a note higher, thus:

Ex. 5

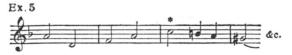

This example is chosen as beginning in the original key: the process began in other keys, and covers the widest range of modulation Bach permits himself in regular fugues.

Bach is not yet ready to display the resources known as 'stretti': but he cannot resist the temptation to indulge in two pairs of a kind of double entry in thirds, syncopated, thus:

Ex. 6

The upper voices overlap with an analogous combination in sixths.

CONTRAPUNCTUS V is the first of three fugues in stretto. A stretto is the overlapping of subject and answer, and the term should not, if *Die Kunst der Fuge* has any authority, be applied (as it often is) to mere fragmentary imitations between the voices, however close these may be. In order to make his theme more plastic Bach now fills out its intervals in a dotted rhythm, thus:

Ex.7

Beginning, as you will hear, with the inverted theme he answers it immediately, in the fourth bar, by the direct theme. Each of the four voices enters twice with one or the other version, before anything remarkable happens. Then the stretti begin. Bach, unlike the writers of text-books, puts the closest foremost. They are always between two parts, greater complexities being reserved for the next fugues: but they are already numerous, an answer being possible at each of the notes marked *. There are two highly effective episodes consisting of close four-part imitations on the main figure of the subject. The first begins thus—

Ex. 8

and the second is its inversion. This is much on the lines of the famous so-called stretti in the Amen Chorus in the *Messiah*. It is hardly what Bach would call a stretto at all, being merely an apposite use of a cliché as old as the art of counterpoint itself. The fugue ends with the subject direct and inverted simultaneously.

The next two fugues are solid masses of stretto from beginning to end, the episodes being mere connective tissue, itself derived from the figures of the theme.

CONTRAPUNCTUS VI is designated *in stile francese* because its jerky rhythms resemble those of the slow introductions to French Overtures. The subject is treated by diminution (i.e., in notes of half the length) as well as by inversion: and the diminution can assert itself several times before one part has accomplished the ordinary subject. The listener should not try to distinguish the twenty-nine or thirty complete entries from the all-pervading tissue of imitations, but should enjoy the natural and smooth growth to a climax.

In CONTRAPUNCTUS VII augmentation (i.e., delivery in notes

of double length) is added to the scheme; and in the general torrent of imitations the theme is also adumbrated as a double diminution in runs such as:

Ex. 9

You need listen only for the augmentations, which boom majestically at long intervals, once in each voice beginning with the bass, and alternately direct and inverted, the final climax being naturally formed by the entry of the direct augmentation in the treble.

Seven fugues have been occupied with setting forth the combinations of the subject with itself. Bach now enters upon the much more important task of combining the subject with other subjects. This is the normal business of the most musical kind of fugue on a large scale; and CONTRAPUNCTUS VIII, which is an essay in triple counterpoint, would from the outset have been recognized as one of Bach's greatest compositions if it had not been put forward as part of a theoretical demonstration. The first thirty-nine bars are given to the exposition and partial development of the following subject:

Ex. 10

It is announced by the middle voice, answered by the bass, and the exposition is completed by the treble. A later entry in the middle voice is imitated in close stretto by the bass. And there is a good deal of delicate contrivance in the local countersubjects and episodic figures, such as:

Ex. 11

Besides a sequential allusion to (*a*) in the treble, there is one more entry of the subject in the bass, which brings this first section to an end at bar 39. The first subject is now combined with a second—

Ex. 12

G

and the pair are now worked out in conjunction with an auxiliary figure (*x*) until bar 93, where, after a considerable climax on the dominant, the third theme-subject appears. It is the inverted motto theme of the whole work in a graceful Brahms-like transformation.

Ex.13

After this has been exposed, the former pair of themes returns with new developments; but the whole triple counterpoint does not appear until bar 147, where the harmony glides in a very remarkable way from A minor to F major.

Ex.14

This begins the final stage of the fugue. With five entries of the triple combination, each of them showing a different position, the harmony straightens itself out towards the firm re-establishment of D minor; and so this final section broadens majestically to its punctual close.

CONTRAPUNCTUS IX, *alla Duodecima*, displays the important resource of double counterpoint in the twelfth. If two or more subjects are to be combined in a fugue, it is necessary that they should be in double or triple counterpoint in the octave. Otherwise it would be impossible to put an upper subject into the bass; but if one or more of a combination of themes can be transposed by some other interval than an octave, we shall get not merely the permutations of the harmonic proposition, but a totally new set of harmonies, besides a certain change of melodic expression in the part that has been specially transposed.

CONTRAPUNCTUS IX exposes a running theme—

Ex.15

which I give in the notation of Bach's first draft. The exposition of this theme is allowed some room to unfold itself, but the fugue runs on without interruption, and the motto theme enters in combination with the running theme as if such incidents were a matter of course.

Ex. 16

Thus, in Bach's original notation, the motto theme appears in its normal size. The alla breve notation of the printed editions is a mere economy for the engravers, as it needs only half the number of strokes to support the runs; but it is apt to give rise to the mistaken idea that the motto theme is augmented (a meaningless notion when the rest of the fugue offers no standard of comparison). When the motto theme comes below the running theme we find that the double counterpoint is in the twelfth. The meaning of this is very evident to the ear, since the combination produces a different balance of key, and the running theme becomes as changed in expression as the aspect of a square that is set up on one of its corners inside of lying flat.

Ex. 17

CONTRAPUNCTUS X, *alla Decima*, displays the nature and purpose of double counterpoint in the tenth. The primary purpose of such counterpoint is not any definite change of harmonic character in the combination taken in itself, but an extensive series of by-products. Nevertheless, Bach has here achieved some very subtle and beautiful harmonic effects akin to those of the old Church modes, by means of the unexpected turns given by the inversions of the pair of themes. But the main purpose of double counterpoint in the tenth is that it enables either or both themes to be doubled in thirds or sixths. Doubling in lower thirds is possible if the double counterpoint is also in the octave. Doubling in upper thirds is possible when the double counterpoint is also in the twelfth. If the composer observes the rules which ensure the working of double counterpoint in the tenth, it probably will work in the octave and twelfth as well, and with the doubling either way of either or both themes. Consequently, such a combination is almost certain to be workable in twenty-four positions, and will probably admit of forty-eight or ninety-six. It is not to be supposed that a composer wastes his time in figuring these all out. Bach does not even trouble to give a position in which both themes are doubled; he prefers to have one part free to complete the harmony in other ways. Nor does he set forth the melodic inversion of the combination, which, if I mistake not, would bring the permutations up to 192, 384, or, for all I care, thousands. Originally, he began this fugue where the motto theme now enters, but he afterwards added the very beautiful first page in which the fugue now begins with its mysterious special subject.

Ex. 18

Inversion

Answer

This is exposed and developed in close stretto by inversion before the inverted motto theme enters.

The motto theme has a separate exposition, and the combined themes are also displayed with their inversions in the tenth before we are given typical combinations in the sixths and thirds.

Ex. 19

But the chief glory of the fugue is in its numerous episodes, which are so various as to sound like expositions of new themes, and enjoyable without worry as to their origins.

CONTRAPUNCTUS XI brings Bach to a crisis which I believe was not foreseen by him, and which led him to extend the plan of the whole work in a surprising way. The intention of this fugue is to turn the three themes of Contrapunctus VIII upside down and, in fact, to demonstrate the total inversion of a piece of triple counterpoint. By a remarkable accident this had never occurred before on any extensive scale in Bach's works. He had often inverted pairs of themes in this total sense—that is to say, inverting the melodies themselves as well as their positions; bu he had never happened to invert more than two at a tim ; and now, when he applies the process to the three themes of Contrapunctus VIII, he encounters the fact that the combination will not work. The discords of the second theme resolve upwards in a harsh and ungrammatical way—in other words, they do not resolve at all. Moreover, the main theme of Contrapunctus VIII was not, like the motto theme, born to be inverted, but when inverted becomes a thing which Bach prefers not to bring often into the top part. So he alters his quaver theme. In general it rises where the original version descended, but the actual discords are made to resolve normally. And, as the fugue is in four parts, Bach adds a fourth figure, consisting simply of a chromatic scale, which digests the awkward and inexact features into beautiful chromatic four-part harmony. He begins the fugue with an exposition and development of the direct motto theme in the rhythm in which it appeared inverted in Contrapunctus VIII. The fugue is clearly divided into sections, punctuated by full closes. The exploitation of the triple counterpoint is by no means the most important feature of the fugue.

Ex. 20   Bar 146

In fact, there are only three appearances of the three themes of Contrapunctus IX thus inverted, the last two being at the end of the fugue. A much more striking feature is the presentation of the motto theme, direct and inverted—the two forms together, not in stretto but quite simultaneous. As this combination happens to be in double counterpoint in the tenth, its reversal gives rise to new harmonies.

Ex. 21
Bar 158   Inversion in 10th   &c.

For a full analysis of the four fugues, Contrapunctus VIII,
IX, X, and XI, I must refer the listener to my *Companion to the
Art of Fugue*. Let me repeat the warning and encouragement
that it is no part of the music-lover's task to attend to any or all
of these contrapuntal complexities at once. The eye has no difficulty in enjoying the changes of a kaleidoscope. Once the symmetry has been secured by a proper setting of the mirrors, the
thing becomes a single impression; and so it is with properly
devised contrapuntal combinations. But here in Contrapunctus XI, Bach has discovered a flaw in the machinery. Aesthetically he puts it right by interfering with the mechanism, but now
he wishes to explore the special mechanism necessary for totally
invertible harmony in more than two parts. This he does by the
drastic process of writing two fugues, or pairs of fugues, which
are totally invertible from beginning to end. The first fugue is
a simple four-part affair on the motto theme, in which the only
special device is an ornamental variation to which it is subjected
soon after the exposition.

Ex.22   Plain Theme

Variation   &c.

Bach prints the *inversus* fugue under the *rectus*, so as to display
a mirror effect. This is amusingly visible, even in short score,
in the last bar.

Ex. 23

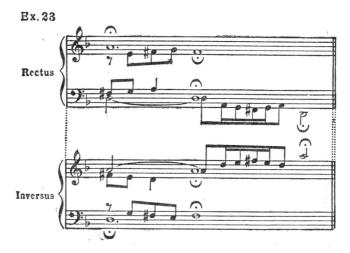

Rectus

Inversus

In the second fugue the parts are turned inside out as well as upside down; top, middle, and bottom of the *rectus* becoming bottom, top, and middle respectively in the *inversus*. You may not perhaps easily recognize until it is pointed out to you that the jaunty theme of this pair of fugues is a variation of the motto theme. The model fugue is itself by inversion, using both forms of its theme.

Ex. 24

Until recently it was thought that the enormous unfinished fugue which stands at the end of *Die Kunst der Fuge* was outside its scheme, since, while its last section has evidently been reached in the combination of three themes with which it breaks off, none of these three themes is the motto theme. Nottebohm, the famous decipherer of Beethoven's sketch-books, discovered that the plain version of the motto theme combines with the other three in the simplest possible manner with a correctness that cannot conceivably be accidental. Independently of other researchers who may have anticipated me, I find that all difficulties in the working of the combination and of its tonal inversion in all four themes will vanish as soon as we realize that the first theme of this fugue is in double counterpoint in the twelfth to the others. That is to say: in the combinations, whenever the direct theme appears in any part but the bass, or the inverted theme in any part but the treble, it must be transposed by a fifth or a twelfth instead of by an octave. The four themes are as follows:

Ex. 25

Direct   Inverted

The first, which I call the canto fermo, is exposed and developed as a complete fugue equal in length to the great C sharp minor in the First Book of the Forty-Eight, with seven stretti, direct and by inversion. The second theme I call the coloratura.

Ex. 26

It has a separate exposition, and its combination with the first theme should already show to a critic wise after the event that there is some difficulty in putting that canto fermo into normal positions except in the bass. The third theme is Bach's own name according to German musical terminology, where B♭ is called B and B♮ is H.

Ex. 27

This brings a chromatic quality into the harmony, which Bach develops with the utmost depth of his imagination. We cannot be too thankful that he lived long enough to produce this section of the fugue. No page in all his works could be so hopelessly beyond conjecture as to general contents and details. He subjects his name to inversion and close stretto with the boldest and most mysterious of harmonies. Then the final stage of this enormous fugue begins, with the three themes in combination. I allowed my pianoforte playing to overlap the last notes of the string-quartet record, so that listeners may have Bach's genuine last notes grafted on to my conjecture as the best justification that can be found for my procedure. My task has been rendered possible by the fact that Bach has placed the whole material before us. Once the listener has disabused himself of the idea that he must attend to all the four threads at once instead of letting the sum-total make its single impression on him, all the essential points will become clear: the new harmonic and melodic angle at which the canto fermo theme stands as soon as it is in an upper part when direct, or in the bass part when inverted: the appearance of the motto theme without interruption to the flow of the others: and the steady climbing of the canto fermo in three continuous steps in the bass, until it is in position after a short pause in the bass to deliver the final stroke that ends the fugue with the motto theme on the top and with Bach's signature as a flourish over the final tonic pedal.

Ex. 28

The Inverted Themes. $\underset{V}{\overset{1}{}}$=The Canto Fermo: $\underset{V}{\overset{2}{}}$ = The Coloratura: $\underset{V}{\overset{3}{}}$ = The Signature: $\underset{V}{\overset{4}{}}$ = The Motto

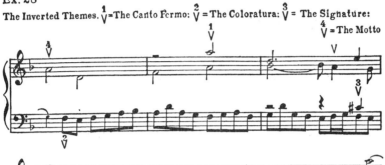

Ex. 29

The Direct Themes, with the Canto Fermo at the 12th

5. TOCCATA IN F SHARP MINOR
(1919)

THIS, the richest and most beautiful of Bach's clavier toccatas, is a very ripe example of his early style; and a good deal of light can be thrown on the problem of its interpretation by the study of the great early Church cantatas, to the period of which it probably belongs. That is to say, where its phrases and forms closely resemble features in such cantatas as *Gottes Zeit* ('God's own time is the best'), *Aus der Tiefe*, and *Christus der ist mein Leben*, we may infer that the words of the cantata indicate the mood of the corresponding passages in the toccata. Nobody, for instance, can suppose that this toccata ends forte if he has once heard the pathetic passage in *Gottes Zeit* where the soprano solo finishes its comment on the hymn of the chorus with the exclamation of a soul welcoming release from earthly life.

I do not mean to imply that this toccata or any of Bach's purely instrumental music is 'descriptive', but to indicate that a composer who is so inveterate and systematic an illustrator of words in his vocal music gives abundant evidence thereby as to the limits within which the player of his instrumental works can assert himself. There is a popular idea, still widely received in the 'pianistic' world, that because Bach gave hardly any marks of expression his music can be fairly interpreted in an unlimited number of contradictory ways; but the truth is more nearly this, that Bach refrained from giving directions, not because he wished to give the player *carte blanche*, but because it was impossible for his contemporaries, with their unavoidable and exclusive knowledge of contemporary idioms, and their peculiarly limited instruments, to play his music in more than one way, if they could play it at all.

The Toccata in F sharp minor is a compendium of all that can be expressed in toccata form. The form arises out of the natural habits of a master of extempore playing when he tries a strange organ, harpsichord, or clavichord. His first action will be to try (*toccare*) the touch of the instrument; accordingly the toccata generally begins with a series of running passages ranging all over the instrument and gathering power and variety as they proceed. Bach inspires these with a dramatic and rhetorical power which idealizes their improvisatorial style. Then, as Bach's early biographer, Forkel, reports, Bach says 'let's see if the instrument has good lungs': and so we have a developed sustained passage in full polyphonic harmony, which in typical cases builds itself up on some figure suggestive of future developments, as in the case now before us:

90

Ex.1

The most brilliant and solid art-form available to the early eighteenth-century composer is the fugue: accordingly after these preliminaries (which give the toccata its title) the music settles down to a lively fugue, presto e staccato.

Ex.2

The great toccata-writers of the late seventeenth century were consummate rhetoricians and sincere artists, but they failed in the power to create a work as a whole. Just as they seem to have settled down comfortably to the fugue their music becomes uneasy or reaches a premature climax; and it accordingly breaks again into the introductory toccata-style, and then tries the fugue once or twice more on the same subject in a new rhythm and time. Out of this interesting but unsatisfactory device Bach, with his supreme mastery of composition, has evolved his great toccata-schemes in as many as four or five complete movements, very various in form, and sometimes (though quite as often not) connected in theme like the sections of a modern symphonic poem. (It is one of the mysteries of musical terminology how such an important form, so suggestive to the modern composer, should in less than a hundred years have given up its name to the dull *perpetuum mobile* études which have since been called toccatas from the time of Clementi to that of Debussy.)

Bach develops his first fugue fully with various episodes, and brings it to a surprising end, which I quote for its own sake and also for the sake of the first bar of the wonderful movement that follows:

Ex.3

New movement (say, Andante)

Here we have an excellent instance of the way in which Bach's music interprets itself as soon as (but not unless) we know the language of his forms. The end of the fugue is simply unplayable without a well-prepared ritardando: while if you gabble through the ensuing glorious page of sequences at the pace suggested by some editors, you may save your respect for Bach by pious platitudes about 'classic reserve and logical severity', but your real state of mind will be that imputed by a former Master of Balliol, Strachan-Davidson, to the schoolboy who 'believes in his heart that no nonsense is too enormous to be a possible translation of a classical author'. For an external proof of the meaning of this glorious page you may turn to the *Christe eleison* of the A major Mass: it is shorter and, like all Bach's later work, much more highly organized; but it leaps to the eye as an emotional utterance. The emotion is not unlike that of this toccata-interlude, and its cumulative method, though shorter and more concentrated, is the same.

The great sequence comes to a climax, accelerates its steps while confining them to the key-note, and at last subsides into the final fugue:

Ex.4

Here you may see the characteristic harking back to an earlier motive (Ex. 1, Figure (*a*)) which makes the toccatas of Buxtehude and Bach seem to foreshadow modern ideas of the 'metamorphosis of themes'.

This fugue, though in four parts, and accordingly very full in harmony, is remarkable for its quiet pathos, not unlike the G sharp minor Fugue in the first book of the *Wohltemperirte Clavier*. But it attains a weighty climax at the end, where it breaks into a final toccata-like cadenza, after which it dies away (as I have already described) in the notes of its own subject.

HAYDN

6. PIANOFORTE SONATA IN E FLAT, NO. I
(1900)

I PROPOSE here to analyse Haydn's largest pianoforte sonata from two points of view. It shall be discussed, in the first place, as if it were an entirely new and difficult work, and, in the second place, it shall be compared with immature works of its own epoch, whereas these show a misleading resemblance to it.

The opening shows that Haydn intends this for a large work:

Ex. 1

In the treatment of the pianoforte within the terms of such art as we have to deal with here, the heavy opening chords imply something unusually grand and broad. Haydn is writing expressly for the pianoforte, but not so as to exclude the performance of his work on the harpsichord. On the harpsichord, what with octave strings and open swell and the peculiarly exciting buzz and rattle produced when many notes are struck at once, this opening would sound very imposing. And on the pianoforte, which Haydn certainly preferred, these thick chords give a very orchestral impression, as contrasted with the light and thin style of writing which the small pianofortes of that time naturally favoured. That light and thin style is just as effective on the modern pianoforte as it was on Haydn's, and the simple device of full chords with a thick but not very deep bass stands in precisely the same relation to it now as it did a hundred years ago; and it is a mere confusion of thought to suppose that because the modern pianoforte obtains still greater and totally different contrasts by totally different means, the contrasts and devices of such writing as keeps to the common ground between the pianoforte and harpsichord can no longer be expressed on the modern instrument. The modern instrument can do all that the early ones did, and if its tone is larger the player must, so to speak, plan his own tone on this larger scale and play his Haydn and Mozart so that they sound as large on the modern pianoforte as they did on their own. And, as we have seen in discussing Bach's harpsichord music, this can only be done by playing the music exactly as it is written; for the written notes, though they do not bring out the full power of the modern instruments, can

93

produce a far greater volume of sound than they could from the old instruments, and any addition to them would destroy the scheme of tone. A rendering that would make them attract our attention while our ears and minds were dulled and satiated with the self-evident contrasts and 'colours' of a Russian symphony or of excerpts from works intended for the modern operatic stage—such a rendering might have a momentary use in awakening us to the forgotten fact that there is colour in Haydn and Mozart, but it would give an utterly false idea of what that colour really is, and, so far from restoring to us our lost sense of fine detail, would only put it farther beyond our reach.

The mature works of Haydn and Mozart are as truly in what Sir Joshua Reynolds calls 'the grand style' as those of Bach and Beethoven, but the grandeur is of proportions not of dimensions, and a 'gigantic' rendering of such things is no less grotesque a travesty than a trivial rendering.

As with the pianoforte-writing, so with the length of phrases. The two bars quoted in No. 1 are the whole of the first theme. The second bar is echoed softly an octave higher, and from it grows a new figure—

Ex. 2

which, after repetition, descends in a long scale down to a third idea, a broad cantabile phrase on an easily swinging semiquaver accompaniment:

Ex. 3

Of this accompaniment, simple as it is, we shall hear strange things in the sequel.

Having stated these three independent items, Haydn welds them together by a counterstatement. It is important for the

understanding alike of classical and of modern music to realize
the principle that true artistic breadth consists in the giving of
unity to a multitude of varied ideas, rather than in merely making
single ideas cover a large space without leaving room for repetition. An artist may easily satisfy his contemporaries by the
latter method; but it is strange to look back on the Dusseks and
Hummels of a hundred years ago, and see how utterly their
'broad melodies' fail to tell, though they are quite excellent in
themselves, and well deserved the admiration they won in their
day. But they have nothing of contrasted proportions to throw
them into relief; and though full of 'character' and 'originality'
in the popular sense (which seems to mean little more than a self-
evident difference from other melodies), they lack that true
originality which consists in a deep knowledge of the meaning
and capabilities of all material that comes to the artist's hands,
whether from without or from within.

Haydn has not, as yet, a use for single melodies that take up
much room; when he has we shall find that their position makes
them more telling than even their obvious breadth and simplicity
would lead one to conceive possible. At present his object is to
indicate that this sonata is a work of noble proportions and rich
material, while he is, nevertheless, plunging instantly *in medias
res*. Hence the above short phrases, treated, by a counterstatement, as if they were a single long phrase. The counterstatement
turns the little demisemiquaver run in the first bar of No. 1,
together with the figure of bar 2, as an impulsive run down
nearly four octaves of scale.

Ex. 4

It is necessary for the organization of quick movements in
terms of this classical art, that there should be as much contrast
in rhythmic motion as can be managed without radical changes
of time. Hence brilliant running passages are certain to occur as
essential parts of the design, and it becomes an interesting problem in criticism to distinguish the cases where such passages are
conventional or diffuse from those where they are really mature
and natural; for their outward appearance and their turns of
phrase are in all cases alike. Here Haydn has settled the question
at once by this impulsive descending scale, thrown in with an
apparent recklessness that gives a new and youthful aspect to his
dignified theme. But from this moment onwards every demisemiquaver passage will inevitably appear to have originated in
this incident. There is now no danger of Haydn's rapid passages

sounding conventional and vapid; a true basis has been provided
for their organic development, and, strange as we may think it,
all rapid scales and flourishes in this movement are, in their way,
as undoubtedly traceable (through No. 4), to the first two bars
of the opening theme as the most striking thematic transformations in, let us say, the first movement of Brahms's Pianoforte
Quintet.

Haydn proceeds with his counterstatement, omitting No. 2 and
giving No. 3 in a higher octave with parts inverted; i.e., the left
hand has the melody and the right hand the semiquaver accompaniment. Here we see the solution of another somewhat
difficult artistic problem. The forms of the classical sonata are
not prima facie contrapuntal, like the forms in which Bach wrote;
indeed a study of the transition from Bach's art to the maturity
of Haydn and Mozart shows that in its early stages modern
musical form was almost incompatible with counterpoint. The
early instrumental works of Haydn and Mozart differ from those
of their contemporaries mainly in the fact that they show a steady
progress in inner contrapuntal life together with extremely
sharply cut form; whereas the Boccherinis and Dittersdorfs
amused themselves and their audiences with experiments on
much more attractive and apparently varied lines but leading to
nothing beyond a 'characteristic style' lacking in permanent
vividness and organic completeness.

In the case of pianoforte solos the antithesis between counterpoint and form evidently gave Mozart and Haydn great trouble,
since in their time the most obvious capabilities of the pianoforte
were such as to distract the composer's and listener's attention
from all polyphonic texture and even from ordinary clear part-
writing. The newly discovered charm of a tone that sings and
yet dies away during all sustained notes; the entirely fresh problems in instrumental part-writing raised by the possibility of
pedal effects; and, in general, the necessity (felt as a serious
problem for the first time in musical history) for working out an
entirely new keyboard technique, starting from that which the
harpsichord and pianoforte had in common, but cautiously going
beyond it wherever new paths showed clearly; all these things
made a contrapuntal style almost impossible. One has only to
look at the work of such an excellent pianoforte stylist as Clementi
to see proof of the strained relation between ordinary counterpoint and early pianoforte technique. Clementi often writes
canonic passages in his sonatas, as a matter of duty; it is (rightly
enough, from some points of view) in his eyes a symptom of
'solid style'. Yet they always disorganize his form, and sound
thin without successfully contrasting with his normal weightier
pianoforte-writing.

Now let us consider Haydn's method in the present case. Here form, counterpoint, and pianoforte style are one. The form already solves the contrapuntal part of the problem, because the phrases are so short that there is no time for a simple accompaniment to pall. In the same way the form, by thus determining what shall be acceptable as accompaniment and inner parts, solves all difficulties as to pianoforte style. We might equally well argue conversely; the pianoforte style and the organization of the inner parts might be said to determine the form. Aesthetically, in the highest art, such as we have here, nothing is logically prior to anything else; the parts determine the whole no less than the whole determines the parts. Technically and historically, no doubt this is not so; in Haydn's case the problem (if he ever thought of it at all except in that highest form of thought that knows no expression short of action) was to make his form determine his texture; just as in Bach's case it would have been exactly the converse.

This may seem a formidable analysis for the first twelve bars of a Haydn sonata; but it is perhaps a sufficient excuse that the principles here stated settle the analysis of the whole sonata, except in matters of key-relationship. Indeed, it may be claimed that we can apply them as a test of the maturity of any work of the same period; and that in a more abstract form they show at least an indication of some vital but not self-evident differences between great and merely successful art of any period. The vitality of art does not depend on the surprising effects it produces: if it did, every living musician would be a greater artist than Beethoven by right of birth and education. It is to the infinite variety *in matters that attract no attention* that we must look for such proof as can be given of an artist's vitality.

The rest of our analysis of Haydn's first movement may be given rapidly with little comment except on the all-important subject of key-relationships. Haydn, having provided in his first twelve bars a rational basis for everything that might otherwise savour of conventionality, makes his counterstatement modulate simply, broadly, and tersely, to the dominant. Here we expect the 'second subject'; but it is a fact which is not as universally understood as one might expect, that with Haydn the first-movement form depends far more on balance of key than on fixed principles of alternation of themes. Haydn in the great majority of cases makes his 'second subject' consist almost wholly of restatements and amplifications of his first, and if he does use a definite contrasted theme there is no foreseeing what he will do with it on recapitulation. His work is on so small a scale that variety, clearness of articulation in phrase, and nobility of proportion will suffice to make it organically complete without the

H

appeals to memory and the more rigid symmetry that are essential to the beauty of later and larger works; and hence it is one of the most mysterious freaks in the history of pedagogy that it should have come to be thought correct to cite Haydn as a typically regular master of form, and Beethoven as a breaker of this regularity. If his sonata forms were nearly as uniform as Beethoven's they would never have impressed the world as beautiful and masterly; for such regularity would have been fatally stiff on such a small scale.

In the present case we see the dividing line between Haydn and Mozart. This sonata, being the largest he ever wrote, is just large enough to make a perfectly symmetrical design desirable and beautiful, but not so large as to allow an absolute line of demarcation between first and second subjects. So Haydn begins his 'dominant' section by further developments of No. 1, the impulsive running treatment given in No. 4 being here turned to account in a more serious though not less brilliant style; and it is not until he has broadened out into a passage of some length and a slightly contrapuntal character, with pianoforte-writing that is very rich for its lightness (note the gorgeous, but carefully high-pitched sforzando chords), that he gives us a new theme, and then it is rather productive of a pleasing surprise at the enlarging of the design than a thing expected as a matter of form.

Ex. 5

As the design enlarges, so does the humour. There is not the least doubt that this is the most hilarious tune in the world. Its continuation is perfectly natural but entirely different in material and rhythm, and leads through a very largely proportioned and dark-toned passage in the minor to a new version of No. 1, more cordial in expression than the original. No. 2 is then brought in to break up the rhythm and thereby enlarge the declamatory emphasis of this passage. Thereon, after a short pause, we have the following 'conventional' resolution—

Ex. 6

which is very telling since it is the first time in the work that such long notes occur. We shall hear more about this in the sequel. The exposition, or first part, ends brilliantly with running passages, and is (like almost all expositions in formal classics) marked to be repeated.

The development, or 'working-out', is introduced by an inversion of No. 6:

Ex. 7

Then we have No. 5 in C major, a somewhat distant key, very fresh and free in its position here as the first modulation to any key other than the dominant. As is natural in development sections, changes of key are frequent as well as free, and we soon find ourselves hurried through F and D minor in demisemiquaver passages akin to those of the first part; until we arrive at a steady imitative episode in semiquavers, on the dominant of G minor:

Ex. 8

This gradually settles down into the semiquaver accompaniment to No. 3, of which the melody soon afterwards appears, also taking shape gradually from subtle and apparently casual suggestions. When it emerges it is treated with bold harmonic effect by being distributed in widely separated octaves in the bass—

Ex. 9

which gives a mysterious power to its chromatic steps.

Then more demisemiquavers, akin to those of the second subject, lead from A♭ (the subdominant) once more to the tonal starting point of the development, the dominant of C, on which, after the longest rapid passage in the whole movement, we once more come to an emphatic pause. Is the development over? And is Haydn going to follow this chord (dominant of the relative minor) by the tonic E♭ as first note of the opening theme, thereby using the harmonic effect so constantly found in old contrapuntal sonatas and concertos whenever a finale follows without break or a slow movement in the relative minor? If this were Haydn's intention, the length and range of his development

would have been exactly what every listener would have expected; but Haydn intends this sonata to surprise us at every
point by its largeness and the nobility of its proportions. Instead
of returning to E♭ he moves in precisely the opposite direction,
to the extremely distant key of E♮. Once more the most hilarious
tune in the world mocks us in this remote region where we have
been led by what has all the appearance of caprice and recklessness. (How deeply artistic and poetical Haydn's design is we
shall first fully appreciate when we have grasped the sonata as
a whole.)

From E we are rapidly taken through A to B minor where
No. 3 is again developed—as always with fresh poetic effect. The
passage lasts just long enough to awaken our expectations of the
establishment of this new distant key, B minor, when suddenly
a magical enharmonic modulation brings us back to the tonic,
E♭, with an abruptness that produces in us a truly amazed realization of the distance we have travelled in this development:

Ex. 10

The recapitulation follows at once without further preparation. The first subject is given exactly as at the outset until the
end of No. 3, which, instead of leading to the counterstatement,
is continued and developed as in No. 9, leading to the chord of
the dominant and so passing back to that version of the first
theme with which the 'second subject' began (if we may give
that name to the whole dominant section of the first part). As
this work is so large and the development has been so surprisingly
wide in its range, Haydn gives us what he is generally not fond
of—a perfectly regular recapitulation. In most cases he prefers
to let his first movement increase in brilliance and elaboration up
to the last line, when, after indulging in passages that develop his
themes in a manner much akin to that of the contrapuntal parts
of some of Beethoven's codas, he rounds off his design by settling
quietly into a reproduction of the cadence-theme of the first
part. But here, where the rest has been so large and free, he
realizes that a more broad and vigorous effect will be produced
by a faithful recapitulation than by any fresh developments.
Indeed, a large expanse of repetition is the one form of expan-
siveness that has not been turned to account before in this
movement.

The only alterations in this recapitulation are, first, a very telling expansion of the incident quoted in No. 6—

Ex. 11

(where the B♭♮ is a truly Beethovenish piece of poetic mystification); and a considerable increase of emphasis and brilliance in the last bars, which enables Haydn to dispense with a coda.

Before proceeding further it is necessary to consider the treatment of distant keys as presented to us in the development of this movement. It is no exaggeration to say that in this respect the present sonata is one of the most interesting compositions in all music. It gives us, in Haydn's terms, a solution of an artistic problem that afterwards remained unattempted in any such difficult form until the later works of Beethoven. And even these do not present a quite obvious parallel to the main feature in Haydn's key-system here. The only obvious parallel that I know is Brahms's Sonata in F major for Pianoforte and Violoncello, and it will throw some light on Haydn's methods if we compare his scheme with that of Brahms. In the first movements of both works we find special and sudden prominence given in the development to the key a semitone above the tonic. Consequently, when both Brahms and Haydn take the astonishing step of choosing this key for the slow movement, the listener's mind has been so far prepared that the effect, though astonishing, is not unintelligible. And in both cases the opening of the third movement in the original tonic owes its characteristic effect to the last chord of the slow movement, though Haydn's device in this matter is much more elaborate than Brahms's. The differences are no less significant than the resemblances. Haydn writes in terms of an art that treats extremely distant keys as mysterious phenomena. His intention is that they shall give to this sonata that impression of unfathomable spaciousness which characterizes all truly poetic art however small its ostensible range. His task is to see that the keys he uses are intelligibly related; but, this done, he needs only to assert them, and it would by no means suit his purpose to demonstrate or even to express their relationship. Let them startle the listener by their capricious and mysterious appearances, and let him feel that they are realities and not accidents, but let them remain mysterious and capricious. A work of art is none the less harmonious and true to nature for embodying mystery and caprice as essential parts of its design.

In later music, from Beethoven's middle period onwards, these

qualities are certainly not on the decline, but extreme key-dis-
tances have become too familiar and their laws too clearly and
constantly in operation for them to be used simply as surprising
effects. There is no large work by Beethoven or Brahms in which
the key-relationships are not firmly systematized, and it may be
safely said that without the expression of such system, a work on
the scale on which Beethoven and Brahms write would fall to
pieces. It is equally safe to say that Haydn's great E flat Sonata
would fall to pieces if its distant keys were expressed as an
explained system.

    That nothing may be wanting to complete the case, Philipp
Emanuel Bach has given us a remarkable foreshadowing of the
present work, in a symphony in D, of which the slow movement
is in E♭. This symphony is musically, as well as historically,
extremely interesting and very effective; but its special claim to
mention here is that it shows so clearly the difference between an
historically interesting experiment and a bold flight of genius.
C. P. E. Bach's slow movement is a lovely little melody, very
picturesquely scored, but there is not the least reason, either in
itself or in its context, why it should have been put in E♭; and
if there were, the effect of the distant key has been weakened
from a shock to a mere wandering, by the insertion of a curious
rhetorical connecting link between the two movements concerned. The passage from the slow movement to the finale is
more mature, and might even have been possible at a later period
than that of Haydn, as far as style and texture are concerned;
but it is one thing to produce modern (or any) effects, and a
very different thing to furnish causes for them.

    Haydn, like Nature and all great artists, has causes for his
effects. If his slow movement gives a strange shock to one's ear
at the first chord, this is entirely in keeping with the strange
blending of humour and solemn sincerity that characterizes the
whole sonata, or indeed the whole man. And the shock of the
first chord at once passes into a strange sense of security and a
touchingly simple solemnity, as Haydn calmly utters the theme
of his slow movement in this most distant of all possible keys:

Ex. 12

The whole movement is derived from the first bar. Statements
of this kind are apt to be inaccurate and misleading; but here it
is a matter that can be settled by rapidly casting one's eye over
the movement, when it will be seen that the form is simply A,

a binary melody with both parts repeated; B, another binary melody in the minor, on the same figure developed—

Ex. 13

but sharply contrasted in character, and without repeats, the second part being, moreover, incomplete so as to lead to A, da capo, with increased ornamentation and three bars of coda derived from inversion of the initial figure, thus:

Ex. 14

Last bar of theme   Coda

The movement needs no further comment. Beauties like the transition through C major in the second part of the theme, and the delicate relief given to the tenderly solemn expression by the curious ornaments (especially in the minor episode in contrast to a sterner tone), and the exquisite finish of the pianoforte-writing, may be left to speak for themselves.

Strokes of genius were more or less a habit with Haydn; but the opening of the finale of this sonata is nothing less than a landmark in aesthetics. The adagio prepared us for its solemnity by the initial shock of its first chord in so distant a key; the finale brings us back to activity—and laughter, by a pretence of explaining away that distant key and all the solemn thoughts it brought. Play a single note after a chord of E major and you will find none that will give so contradictory an effect as G♮. E♭, unaccompanied, would sound like D♯ and be interpreted by the ear as third of the dominant chord. B♭ would also be taken for A♯, as third in a chord modulating to the dominant key. But G♮ suggests nothing but a definite contradiction of the third of the E major chord, its synonym, F♯♯, having no essential harmonic meaning in such a context.

So when the finale begins by gently tapping G♮ in this rhythm

one's momentary impression is that the key is E minor. This is at once drastically corrected by the bass, which enters on E♭

thus showing the real key of the theme, which proves to be a simple phrase on tonic and dominant harmony (over a tonic pedal). But this is not more than half of Haydn's artistic device. G♮ has given a shock to ears that have just been listening to a final chord of which the most sensitive note was G♯. Then G♯, or something scarcely distinguishable from it in pitch, shall be shown in a new light. The opening phrase is repeated a step higher, on the supertonic, so that it now begins by gently tapping A♭—a note practically (and, on a pianoforte, absolutely) identical with G♯, but of course here unmistakable as third of the supertonic in E♭. This done, the bass bursts out fortissimo on the dominant with the same theme, the treble having a brilliant running counterpoint.

We have seen how the opening of the first movement contained a solution for all the problems Haydn had to face in writing solos for the pianoforte. The opening of the finale is no less compendious. The theme begins with a purely rhythmic figure on one note. If this rhythm is treated as an accompaniment (and Haydn so treats it from the outset), that accompaniment is *ipso facto* alive and thematic, even though it is so simple that the most ordinary non-thematic accompaniment sounds almost elaborate in comparison—as we observe early in the development section. It is interesting to note that Beethoven, in his 'second period', developed a strong predilection for such rhythmic figures in his themes, and used them constantly as a most powerful means of giving life to inner parts without the necessity for the counterpoint, which would have sounded restless and obtrusive against the broadly designed contrasts and developments that he was executing. In his later work, when he once more found a constant use for melodic counterpoint, he relied much less on rhythmic figures, except in extremely large works like the Ninth Symphony.

To return to Haydn and conclude this attempt at sketching a few leading principles in his art: the finale needs no detailed analysis if these principles are grasped. The object of this analysis has not been to help us to follow Haydn, but to help us to listen to him. If he were more difficult to follow, he would be more often and more easily listened to. The reader will observe that there is little enough analysis of form in this essay; and what there is covers the ground fairly completely. In stating that the finale is in ordinary first-movement form, that it does not go into distant keys, that all its themes are derived from its opening rhythm except a brilliant arpeggio passage in the second subject, that the preparations for the return of the first theme constitute one of the most extravagantly comical passages Haydn ever wrote, and that there is no coda—in stating these things I have given a complete analysis of the movement, an analysis that is probably just as useful as most of its kind: but what concerns the modern listener is not these bare facts but their reasons. It does not concern us merely to know that Haydn avoids distant keys, but it intimately concerns us that we should feel that he avoids them because he is restoring balance after an extremely bold venture into extreme distance. It does not much avail us to recognize that the rapid passages in the development are suggested partly by the running counterpoint to the first theme and partly by the arpeggio showers in the second subject, if we fail to enjoy Haydn's splendid audacity in spending twenty-seven bars steadily in the tonic when, according to all the ordinary rules of form and all that one would naturally expect at such a stage of the development, he ought to be going from key to key, avoiding the tonic as a thing reserved for the formal return of his theme. After he has with equal nonchalance swerved aside into another key and come to a pause, the comical chromatic return has a greater depth and truth in its humour if we have appreciated its context, than if we see in it merely such a piece of *badinage* over a chromatic scale as is used merely to raise a laugh by every ordinary writer of comic operas at all epochs.

Neither Haydn nor Mozart succeeded in writing many mature pianoforte solos of such importance as this sonata. The problems involved therein were too delicate and difficult to be attacked by more methodical means than such happy inspirations as occur seldom in a great man's lifetime. Hence the majority of Haydn's and Mozart's mature instrumental works are for combinations of instruments where polyphony can exist without disturbing the individual technique of the instruments; and when ordinary polyphonic methods are possible, the problems of giving life to the inner texture are already half solved. But Haydn's and Mozart's solo works are thus only the more original and subtle in the rare cases where they attain artistic maturity; and it is an experience with which all investigators are familiar, that the more singular a problem appears, the richer its solution is likely to be in principles that stimulate and enlighten.

MOZART

Largo (C), leading to *Allegro Moderato*, E flat major, C.
Larghetto, B flat major, 3/8.
RONDO, *Allegretto*, E flat major. ¢,

THE world is older than it was in the days when the 'Romanticists' were uttering their well-timed protest against the pedantries of an uncritical age. We have learned to understand Schumann, and we know that he was no less deeply familiar with classical music than Milton was with classical scholarship; and we realize, or ought to realize, that the reactionary element in the 'Romantic' school was one of reaction, not against Mozart and Haydn, but against the formulas of those who blindly worshipped the Mozart of the pianoforte sonatas and the masses, and who shrewdly suspected that the composer who had advanced the art of music since Mozart's death was not Beethoven but Hummel.

The cause of Schumann has triumphed, and we know that besides being the great 'Romantic' seer, he was one of the most learned contrapuntists that ever lived, so we may turn to the serious study of Mozart (as Schumann himself did) with minds undistracted by any vague fears of writing ourselves down asses and pedants. To complete our advantage, the chronology and canon of Mozart's works is accessible to every one. Köchel's great chronological catalogue of numbers is adopted in every edition or citation of Mozart's works—no one need any longer base a serious estimate of Mozart's tendencies and development on his masses (written at Salzburg to the order and specification of that notorious Archbishop under whose régime Mozart had to dine in the kitchen, and was kicked out of the room by the steward when he asked for an increase of salary) or on his pianoforte sonatas—written, so to speak, with his left hand while his right was engaged in those colossal works *Idomeneo* and *Entführung*. When, to crown all, Mozart himself is found to have inscribed some of his best known solo sonatas 'for a beginner', we cannot but feel that it is truly amazing that the solo sonatas and masses should contain any of the beautiful and interesting things that we actually do find in them: indeed, the accidents that have brought his hack-work into such disproportionate prominence ought, so far from proving unfortunate, only to make us realize more clearly than ever how indomitable is the courage of a man with great and real ideals.

Let us, then, abandon futile attempts to put Mozart on a lower plane than that of the greatest composers. We have learnt to realize that Palestrina is one of the greatest, though we well know that the slightest modern musical lyric has a far wider range of resource and feeling. But the feeling is not more true or deep, nor is it more the whole truth within its range. The artist of greater range is on the same plane as the artist of narrower range, provided the range is in both cases the widest that the development of the art will allow, and provided also that that development is such as to admit the production of really mature masterpieces. We have learnt to appreciate and act on these principles in forming our estimate of Palestrina; and probably we have been much helped in this case by the fact that Palestrina was succeeded by three generations of men who worked in the dark, so that the perfection and power of his art is borne in on us by the utter inability of his more ambitious successors to produce anything that could stand beside it. In the case of Mozart, we find that Beethoven immediately followed him by equally perfect work of vastly wider range; but though this makes Beethoven a vastly greater composer, still that is a strange confusion of thought that would make us put Mozart on a lower intellectual plane, as if the perfection of a work could be affected by the subsequent production of totally different works on a much larger scale.

Mozart is not a specialist like Chopin, one who uses the resources of an enormously comprehensive art for the working-out of a single closely limited province; nor is he a great genius born, like Purcell, to work in an age when the art was not ripe for perfect organization. He is a supreme master over the whole resources of what was, in his time, the complete and mature art of music; he did all that so short a lifetime has ever been known to achieve in the way of extending those resources without disorganizing the art; and unless we are to suppose that truth, wisdom, and artistic greatness are matters of quantity rather than quality, so that the average schoolboy is more highly cultured than an Athenian of the days of Pericles, and every student who erects an apt conjunction of chromatic passing-notes and bass clarinets into a correct symphony is a greater composer than Bach and Beethoven, it is at least doubtful whether those who would deny Mozart his place among the greatest of all time really have any logical ground to stand on.

At all events, it can do us no harm to make a serious attempt to understand this wind quintet, though it is one of the simplest works in his most mature style. If we feel inclined to regard its emotional expression as childlike (a quality in which, for all its evenness and simplicity, it does not radically differ from even the most tragic of great artistic creations), we shall do well to recall our own childhood for a moment, in order to realize that where we were not spoilt or affected little prigs, our emotions were as true and intense as any that we can know later, though their range was so small.

This quintet ought to help us more easily than most to realize Mozart's greatness; not that it is greater than his other mature works, but because it is written for a very unusual combination of instruments, so that the strange conditions and limitations of Mozart's present material give us those clues to a great artist's cunning which cannot be detected by researches in works produced with more plastic resources. Not that there is the least sign of awkwardness or artificiality in the present work. If we did not know to the contrary, we should see no reason to suppose that Mozart did not write three works for the same combination every year of his working life; but when we know what the practical difficulties of the combination must be, and when we turn to Mozart and find that he solves every one of them by turning them into so many means of beautiful and appropriate effect, then it may occur to us that this art which the strange conditions have made manifest really exists in far more varied and subtle developments in Mozart's works for ordinary combinations, since those combinations are ordinary just because they give better opportunities to the composer.

It seems strange that writers on musical aesthetics have not studied the extraordinary number of works for strange and unpromising combinations that Mozart has left us. No other composer has given half as many opportunities of seeing revealed by strange conditions the art which is so thoroughly concealed by genius. Among such works are Divertimenti for two flutes, five trumpets, and four drums (unimportant music, but written with a smoothness that would have suggested years of experience and familiarity with the combination, if the very idea were not absurd); a very graceful and enjoyable Concerto for flute and harp—his pet aversions among musical instruments; or, to turn to really powerful and profound artistic creations, several pieces for a musical clock, which have been transferred to a place among the finest items in the repertoire of modern organists; and, loveliest of all these smaller freaks, an Adagio and Rondo for flute, oboe, viola, violoncello, and *glass harmonica*, which makes one simply long to have a proper glass harmonica made and to learn it oneself without delay, for the express purpose of getting up a serious performance of this exquisite thing.

But none of these extraordinary works is so large and important as this quintet. True, it is not the only one by a great composer for the same combination; for there is one in the same key, and obviously on the same plan, by Beethoven. But this is just the final link in our chain of evidence, for this work of Beethoven's is one in his 'first period'; and not only that, but it represents the cautious and imitating aspect of that period. It is too little remembered that what is called Beethoven's 'first period' contains at least three distinct styles: first, the cautious Mozart-esque Beethoven of the Wind Quintet, the Septet, and other such works; secondly, the true unmistakable Beethoven, terse, vigorous, and intensely original, but working on a small scale, the Beethoven of the Sonata in A major, op. 2, no. 2; and thirdly the combination of these two, Beethoven the young and ambitious, eager to write on a larger scale than Mozart, but not always completely furnished with the new resources that are necessary for the carrying out of his larger schemes—Beethoven, as we see him in the C major Sonata, op. 2, no. 3, or the first movement of the F major Violoncello Sonata.

Beethoven's Quintet for pianoforte and wind belongs to the second of these early styles, but shows traces of the ambitious element. And as it throws a flood of light on Mozart, I shall frequently cite the Beethoven Quintet to show how Mozart solves problems that Beethoven, in his imitation of Mozart, hardly so much as perceived. We have grown so accustomed to comparing Mozart and Beethoven to the detriment of the former, that it will be a healthy novelty to turn the tables for once: especially if we bear in mind that Beethoven's Wind Quintet, one of the least characteristic of all his works, is exceedingly beautiful, and that the gulf between it and ordinary academic composition is incomparably greater than the gulf between Mozart's Quintet and it.

Mozart's introduction is a perfect realization of all that is best calculated to make the introduction to a beautiful and nobly-proportioned work as stately as possible. For this purpose, nothing can be more telling than short phrases that admit of piling up into long sequences. A short phrase repeated in various positions eight times will weigh far more on the mind than a single phrase of eight times the length, and, moreover, when a longer phrase is introduced as a contrast to such sequences, it has a vastly larger effect than if it were surrounded with things of the same length.

Mozart begins his introduction by making the best of both methods at once. His first motive is a group of sequences on the following figure—

Ex. 1

which he rounds off in the guise of a four-bar melody, and follows by an expanded counterstatement. Beethoven begins his introduction with material which, though beautiful, and containing an incidental sequential touch, is felt simply and solely as a four-bar melody, with an unexpanded counterstatement. So that Mozart's first nine bars, as compared with Beethoven's, contain six complete sequential repetitions (besides subordinate ones), together with all Beethoven's impression of broad melodic articulation, with the additional breadth of an expansion in the counterstatement. Furthermore, Mozart has so divided his dialogue that all the instruments have already appeared in these nine bars both as individuals and as tutti; whereas Beethoven's undivided melody has only admitted of the contrast of pianoforte and the whole mass of the wind quartet.

After this Mozart continues with a pile of sequences on the following simple figure:

Ex. 2

When this has passed through the five instruments in rising succession we think we have reached the end of an unusually persistent sequence (most sequences are abandoned after three steps, at least so we are told when we write exercises), but no! it has not occurred forte in the bass and with fresh matter on the surface; so Mozart promptly makes it do so for three more steps, and after these magnificent eight steps, the rhythm breaks, and we find ourselves on a dominant pedal—in suspense for some splendid allegro to come. On this pedal a new phrase is uttered by the clarinet—

Ex. 3

and this again continues for no less than six steps without any suspicion of monotony. The introduction draws slowly and grandly to its close on a dominant pause; it is one bar shorter than Beethoven's and contains these three huge sequential piles!

The allegro moderato opens with a cantabile melody—

Ex. 4

which loses none of its breadth from the fact that within eight
bars we have two alterations from quiet solo to forte tutti, and
a complete statement and counterstatement. Beethoven's allegro
also begins with a beautiful cantabile, but one that is for pianoforte alone, and more than twice the length of Mozart's eight
bars before the wind instruments enter with the counterstatement
at all. Now, observe the practical and artistic advantages of
Mozart's material and method. Wind instruments need much
consideration in the providing of breathing spaces; they cannot,
like a violin, continue for pages together without stopping; and
indeed they need not only spaces in which to catch a breath, but
from time to time longer rests, in which the player may draw
many long breaths and take the strain off his lips altogether. No
one knew this better than Beethoven; but the long undivided
themes of his wind quintet oblige him to make the necessary rests
take the form of equally long silences, while the pianoforte
indulges in full statements and counterstatements.

That this is not altogether satisfactory to Beethoven himself
is proved by the fact that when he arranged the work as a quartet
for pianoforte and strings he inserted additional accompaniments
for the strings in at least the latter portions of every one of these
long rests. It is thus clear that he did not feel that the giving of
long solos to one instrument after another was the highest ideal
of instrumental polyphony, though it was the only thing that
wind instruments could do with these long indivisible themes.
Compared with this, Mozart shows himself in a state of development which we find in vastly larger and deeper conceptions in
the works of Beethoven's 'third period'. Consider, once more,
how the intensely characteristic and salient tones of wind instruments are likely to pall when heard too continuously, and see
how immensely it is to Mozart's advantage, not only that his
work should be shorter, but that his themes should be so
minutely divided among the instruments that we never hear
two bars together in the same quality of tone.

Mozart follows his first theme by a crowd of subsidiaries, all
moving very tersely (most of them shorter than the bars, so that
a bar-stroke is by no means an infallible indication of where the
accent falls), and culminating in a very brilliant tutti founded on
No. 2, the only allusion Mozart makes to the introduction—

Ex. 5

Oboe
Clarinet
Horn

Pianoforte

unless we count a probably accidental resemblance—

in the passage on the dominant of B flat which follows it and leads to the second subject.

In the second subject we may again profitably contrast Mozart's splendid and rapid variety and terseness with the beautiful but uniform and uneconomical pianoforte cantabile the ambitious Beethoven puts in the corresponding place in his quintet. Here are two bars of Mozart's first member of the second subject:

Ex.6

As in the opening theme of the allegro, statement and reversed counterstatement are disposed of in eight bars with a manner which has no suggestion of anything less leisurely than a most dignified breadth. This theme is followed by a brilliant running theme for the pianoforte alone; it being now time, according to Mozart's methods, that some such solo passage should appear as a contrast to the close dialogue we have had so far.

Ex.7

In relation to the rapidity of Mozart's action, three and a half of these long bars are quite sufficient to round the passage off, and to give the wind instruments a very satisfactory breathing space. And then Mozart has ample time to give a counterstatement of this passage so ingeniously varied that if it occurred in a modern theme in a work of Brahms, half the analysts would say it was a new theme, while the other half would say that 'it would seem on close investigation to be derived—perhaps somewhat obscurely —from the former theme'. However, as we fondly imagine that we are thoroughly familiar with Mozart's style, such incidents in his work are recognized at once, and regarded as ridiculously simple. Here is his counterstatement—

Ex.8

during which the pianoforte has a complete rest—a thing that never happens in the Beethoven Quintet. Moreover, Mozart greatly expands his counterstatement, evading the full close of the first version, and erecting two short piles of sequences passing through the five instruments, and securing that breadth and massiveness that we saw so clearly typified in the introduction. The whole passage is perhaps the finest example of the way in which this quintet surpasses Beethoven's imitation of it. Beethoven, following Mozart step by step, also had at the same point in his movement a brilliant theme for pianoforte solo, but he makes it so long that it is impossible to keep the wind instruments silent all the time, so that they have to find something to do, though they have no other reason than that for throwing in their humorous comments. Of course, a counterstatement—not to speak of an expanded one—is absolutely out of the question.

Mozart, after working out his brilliant subsidiary in so splendid and unexpectedly large a manner, concludes his exposition with a group of cadence-figures, of which I quote the last:

Ex.9

The first part (i.e., all from the beginning of the allegro) is repeated.

The development begins by repeating the last cadence figure (No. 9) on G. Beethoven does precisely the same in his quintet, but as his cadence-figure is fortissimo the effect is formal to a degree which Mozart shows only in much earlier works than the present—works such as the 'Paris' Symphony or the main bulk of the pianoforte sonatas.

The present development is one of the shortest for its value ever written, and for telling simplicity, unity, and subtlety stands without a rival among short developments until we come to that of the first movement of Beethoven's Sonata 'Les Adieux', which reads almost like some immensely profound and emotional paraphrase of it.

I

Mozart's development is founded entirely on rising and falling sequences on the first two bars of the movement (No. 4). It is only sixteen bars long; but there is extraordinary breadth in the effect of the theme being carried up in four long steps of rising sequence, and then a small figure from it (see bar 2 of No. 4) being carried down in a falling sequence of eight short steps to close quietly in the tonic with a resumption of the full theme as at the outset of the movement. And there is something strangely deep and beautiful in the effect of the place, half-way through the development, where the instruments all join in a quiet statement of two bars of the theme in C major, the most distant and brilliant key touched on in the whole movement.

Among the many extraordinary fallacies that are rife as to the methods of Haydn and Mozart, none is more startling than the notion that they are extremely regular and exact in their recapitulations. With Haydn the second subject is, more often than not, represented by altogether strange and new processes of development; and though with Mozart the second subject is, as in the present instance, closely reproduced, the first subject is often treated quite as freely as it is in Beethoven. In the present instance Mozart, taking advantage, no doubt, of the opportunities given by the shortness of his development portion, makes the counterstatement of his first theme pass into a new passage of six bars of sequential treatment of the first figure (see first bar of No. 4), thus making the recapitulation seem almost to carry on the short development and add to its breadth and weight. When these things happen in Brahms, we say 'How obscure!' This passage proves a short cut to the brilliant transition-theme, No. 5, and a further short cut brings us from thence straight to the second subject in the tonic. The framework of this is, as I have said before, unaltered; but there is plenty of matter for attention in the manner in which the material is redistributed among the instruments so as to produce entirely fresh combinations of tone. The finest instances of this are the delightful moment when the horn discovers that the main second-subject theme (No. 6) lies in the very best part of what was in Mozart's time its exceedingly incomplete and uneven scale, and the cadence figures, where the pianoforte and wind change parts and there is some splendidly bright and kaleidoscopic colouring.

There is no coda, but the final cadence (No. 9) is insisted on and expanded, while the pianoforte and horn each throw in a jubilant arpeggio. Beethoven in his coda also took care to give a rapid arpeggio to the horn, but in order to work it in he had to drop thematic and organized structure altogether, and break up the movement with a long cadenza. We shall see in the

finale how Mozart manages to make a long free cadenza the very
means of pulling the structure together.

Turning now to the slow movement, we begin to leave the
close textures that we have seen in the first movement. It is an
obvious aesthetic principle that a work should become easier to
follow as it proceeds; not less interesting or serious, but more
readily engaging the attention by simpler and more salient means
of effect. But Mozart makes this process a gradual one. It is
still a characteristic difference between Mozart's slow movement
and Beethoven's, that Mozart's should be in the same 'binary'
form as the first movement, while Beethoven's is in the easier
and looser rondo form. Still, the differences are not now so
much to the disadvantage of Beethoven; his more diffuse texture
does not appear nearly so much like missing opportunities when
he comes to the later movements of the work, where rigid and
unbroken lines are more appropriate than in a first movement.

Mozart still shows us a splendid variety in his opening theme,
with its alternations between solo and tutti, and its power to
dispense with the pianoforte—

Ex. 10

as compared with Beethoven's eight bars of beautiful cantabile
for pianoforte alone. After the counterstatement Mozart proceeds slowly through various keys, in dialogue between the wind
instruments, with a flowing pianoforte accompaniment. The
dialogue is not at all rapid; each instrument says its say for two
bars and remains silent while its successor answers. Mozart
gives no opportunity for any one to say that he has neglected
those more obvious effects in which Beethoven's Quintet is so
profuse. He only places them so that they will sound fresh and
telling. This passage lands in the dominant (F major), where
the instruments all join, and come slowly and with tender
solemnity to a close. The second subject, so long delayed, is a
single four-bar phrase—

Ex. 11

promptly repeated in free canon thus—

Ex. 12

Clarinet

Pianoforte

&c.

and concluded by a simple cadence-figure passed through the instrument.

The development is entirely episodic; that is to say, it is not founded on the themes of the exposition. After seven bars of preparation (seven bars in this slow tempo produce an effect of very protracted suspense) the horn begins a large theme in three-bar rhythm in E flat (the subdominant).

Ex 13   Oboe

&c.

The continuation of this modulates in a long sequence, the foundation of which may be heard in the bass of the pianoforte descending for no less than nine steps. At the last step an utterly unexpected turn in the harmony lands us in E minor, of all existing keys the most remote from our tonic B flat. Here the pianoforte has some agitated ejaculatory phrases of very dramatic character, while the wind sustains soft chords—the one instrumental effect which we have not been prepared to expect. The harmonic process that underlies this passage is so wonderful and eventful that I quote it here without the crowning pianoforte part:

Ex. 14 a

So far so good; now repeat this a tone lower:

Ex. 14 b

What is that third chord? It is a 6/4 in B flat, our tonic. Mozart calmly closes into the full recapitulation of the first subject (with

fresh ornamentation). The effect of this long and entirely episodic development, receding to what seems an infinite distance
from both the main key and the main theme, and then swooping
in a single smooth harmonic process back to the recapitulation,
is truly immense, and probably owes much of its strength to the
very fact that it is so purely episodic. Also the absence of thematic
working-out happily differentiates this slow movement as an
easier and more free organism than the first movement, striking
a just mean between the developed binary form and the lighter
rondo form which Mozart is reserving for the finale.

There is little more to be said of this wonderful movement.
After that startling development it is, of course, right that the
first theme should be faithfully reproduced, unaltered except for
increased ornamentation. The ensuing dialogue, naturally, has
to take a different course in order to remain in the tonic; and, as
we have now learnt to expect, Mozart takes his opportunity of
working in another huge expansion—but I shall not enter into
details. The reader is doubtless tired of so much talk of 'broad
sequences and expansions', but my object will be accomplished
if his weariness of this talk drives him to take the right pleasure
in the broad sequences themselves.

The counterstatement of the second subject (see No. 12) is, on
recapitulation, in three-part instead of two-part canon. There is
no coda, the movement ending exactly as did its exposition.

With the finale comes Mozart's legitimate opportunity of indulging in the simple effects which characterize the whole of
Beethoven's Quintet. Every form of luxurious ease and light-
heartedness is here, from themeless sustained passages such as
that at the end of the development of the slow movement—but
without the touch of melancholy—to the extraordinary cadenza
in tempo towards the end, and the downright 'excellent fooling'
of the last page. Beethoven in his Quintet never gives himself
half so free a hand as Mozart in this finale, though there is not
a bar in the whole movement that is not as terse and appropriate
as anything in the rest of the work.

The typical form of which this movement is a free example
is a compound between the principles of the rondo and the
'binary' movement, thus—First Subject in tonic; followed by
Second Subject, in dominant; then, instead of development,
First Subject in tonic again; fresh episode in some new key, or
perhaps (where there is closer approximation to the style of a
first movement) a kind of free development of the old material
mixed or unmixed with new; then First Subject again in tonic,
with Second Subject also in tonic (as in a first movement); then
final reappearance of First Subject, and a coda.

Mozart uses this form in the present instance with considerable freedom, as we shall soon see. He begins with the rondo theme, a square eight-bar melody for pianoforte, opening thus:

Ex. 15

This is repeated by the wind, and followed by an important subsidiary, also piled up sequentially into an eight-bar phrase and repeated by the wind:

Ex. 16

The repetition of this, however, quickly carries us to the dominant, where after some preparation and a triplet passage for the pianoforte—

Ex. 17

we have the second subject:

Ex. 18

The continuation of this brings a crowd of short cadence-themes, none of which occurs again, except for a grotesque kind of pumping accompaniment for the bassoon, and afterwards, still more humorously, for the horn—

Ex.19

which we hear in later developments with fresh matter on the top.

At last the rondo theme (No. 15) returns, after long anticipation, in the tonic. It is simply stated in its bare length of eight bars, without counterstatement or subsidiary, and is immediately followed by the next episode, which begins with a new melody, also in regular eight-bar rhythm, in C minor:

Ex. 20

The delightful effect of the horns entering in close imitation of this phrase in the fifth and sixth bars will strike every hearer. After this has been built up into sixteen bars of a 'binary' tune, we plunge into a long, themeless passage, as one might plunge into a dark wood. The winds have sustained notes which, as the sequences bring about perpetual crossing and recrossing of parts, change in tone-quality at every step. The pianoforte has triplet passages which, since they are triplets, have some faint suggestion of the transition-figure (No. 17). At last we come out into daylight and the dominant of E flat. The bassoon and horn betake themselves to the grotesque pumping accompaniment (No. 19), and everything clearly leads back to the first theme. One can almost hear Mozart laughing in his sleeve as he calmly passes through the old transition-passage (No. 17) to the second subject (No. 18) instead. Not a note do we hear of the first subject. On the other hand he entirely neglects the sequel of the second, but after stating its principal eight-bar theme he startles us by deliberately giving out the subsidiary to the first subject, No. 16. He even begins its counterstatement, but at the fifth bar breaks out in an imposing tutti, which eventually culminates in a pause on a 6/4 chord:

Truly this movement is full of surprises. This looks very like preparing for the end, but surely it is much too soon! We have only had eight bars recapitulation of the second subject, and none whatever of the first, and the movement has been so far less than half the length of the first movement. Be this as it may, Mozart sets about writing a long cadenza in tempo, a passage in which the five instruments seem to extemporize together, with no definite allusions to themes—except for triplets in the pianoforte that unmistakably resemble the transition passage No. 17, besides, of course, reminding us of the long passage in the latter part of the C minor episode. If that passage felt like plunging into a dark wood, this cadenza feels like finding one's way through an enormous park, where avenue, glade, and copse bewilder us in their endless succession, and vistas open suddenly before us just when we think the prospect is closing in. Mozart carries on this cadenza in grand piles of sequence of much the same kind (though so different and so light-hearted) as those we found in the introduction to the first movement; till at last the oboe settles down on the final trill, and just as all is over the pianoforte drops quietly into the long-lost rondo theme! The freaks and omissions of the recapitulation, and the suspense caused by this enormous cadenza, combine to give the return of this first theme far more weight and effect than could conceivably have been achieved by other means. Mozart has secured extreme terseness in the body of the movement by these means, together with the utmost lightness and openness of texture. And by the very same means he has contrived to give this finale the grandest and noblest possible proportions; proportions that astound us by revealing themselves at last as being incomparably larger than we expected at the outset. To complete these proportions Mozart has only to celebrate the return of the long-lost first theme, by singing a song to a tune we have not as yet heard even in this happiest of works—the tune of absolute relaxation, when all tasks are triumphantly finished, and the greatest of men may rest on his laurels and enter into the keen delights of Nonsense. The pianoforte begins an absurd figure, such as Mozart used later in *Cosi fan tutte*, where Despina, the maid-servant, disguised as a notary, reads a sham marriage contract in a high monotone, the solemnity of which is belied by occasional ludicrous variations of pitch and rhythm and by our knowledge that the strangers who are parties to the contract are the rightful lovers in disguise.

Ex. 21

Here, however, there is no *arrière pensée*; the wind instruments remain as grave as happy children absorbed in a glorious game, until at last the horn takes to a leisurely pumping, somewhat suggestive of No. 19—but in crotchets. At this the work comes to an end.

Mozart wrote to his father after the first performance of this quintet, that he thought it the best thing he had ever done. He was right then; but it stands early in the noble series of his most mature works of chamber music; and if it presents more handles for aesthetic analysis than its successors that is not because it is finer—for it certainly is not—but because, as we saw at the outset, its unusual combination of instruments gives us so many clues as to those resources which are even more wonderfully and variously used in Mozart's later works for strings and for orchestra.

8. ADAGIO IN E MAJOR FOR VIOLIN (KÖCHEL'S CATALOGUE, NO. 261)
(1900)

THE exquisite A major Violin Concerto of Mozart is an early work, as far as Mozart's true maturity is concerned, but it is the last of his violin concertos; for the much played one in E flat, which stands later in Köchel's Catalogue, was believed by Joachim and others who have troubled to make a close study of its very unfinished part-writing and muddled form to be either spurious or mysteriously garbled.

Why Mozart so soon gave up the writing of violin concertos is not easy to tell. He certainly produced, in his A major Concerto, a most delightful and characteristic work, full of wit and humour, and containing several very bold and effective innovations in form. Nevertheless, he wrote no more concertos for one violin and orchestra, though he was as yet only beginning the long line of his really great instrumental works, and these concertos were his first perfect masterpieces.

A year or so after he wrote the A major Concerto, a certain violinist, Calzabigi by name, played it for him at a concert, and Mozart wrote a new slow movement for the occasion. This new movement is, almost certainly, the Adagio now under consideration, but it shows a decided change of style and is much less suitable as a slow movement to the A major Concerto than was the original one which it thus temporarily displaced. One must remember that while Mozart himself would be sensitive enough over the coherence and contrast of a scheme of movements as embodied in a concerto, his audiences were so far ignorant of the bare possibility of any such idea that in concerts under Mozart's own direction it was considered proper and advisable to do the first movement of a concerto in the first part of a programme, then to proceed to entirely different works, and to put the slow movement and finale somewhere in the second part! Indeed, such bewildering proceedings survived later than the time of Chopin, who treated his own concertos in the same barbarous fashion. If we consider this state of things, it is not difficult to understand how Mozart, brought into contact with a fine violinist who was ready to play his last year's concerto at a certain concert, should find himself inclined to write a new slow movement more specially suited to throw into relief that violinist's qualities of broad tone and cantabile style. The unity of the concerto as a whole was at that time a matter for artists and music-lovers to appreciate in private; the conditions of public performance in any case hopelessly destroyed the impression of unity, and so Mozart would, on the whole, be taking the most artistic course

121

in writing a new and solemn movement which should specially suit the player, rather than in retaining for that particular occasion the original witty and happy movement that was so exactly in keeping with the first movement and finale, but perhaps would not give Calzabigi a fair chance of revealing the dignity of his style. And when this occasion was past the concerto would still be extant in its original form while the new movement became, what we now take it to be, an independent work of great beauty and distinctly later style.

It is strange that this Adagio is so seldom played. It has, fortunately, been in print since 1881 if not earlier, and so is accessible to every one.

It is scored for a very small orchestra, merely strings, two flutes, and two horns; but the violins are muted while the lower strings and the solo-violin are not, and the flutes and horns are so effectively treated that the effect with a proper and properly-handled orchestra is rich and beautiful beyond any idea that can be obtained from hearing the work with pianoforte accompaniment. It would, however, be worth while hearing it with the pianoforte if only to stimulate interest and curiosity as to the full glory of the work; and after all it is only decadent works that are actually dull and unintelligible when stripped of orchestral colours.

The Adagio is in that simple binary form, with a broadly declamatory style which is characteristic of the earlier type of sonata-form slow movement. The opening theme—

Ex 1

is stated by the muted violins with flutes brightening the tone in the higher octave. The unmuted solo violin, entering, after four bars, with a counterstatement, brings a contrast of tone which is enhanced by the temporary absence of the basses.

The second subject is particularly beautiful in orchestral effect:

Ex. 2

Above we have the muted orchestral violins; between them and the swinging staccato bass (or rather in the midst of the bass, for it is doubled in the *upper*, not the lower octave) the unmuted violas on their lowest string; and in the midst a sustained note for the horns that gives fullness and body to the muted violins while adding a new contrasting element of tone. As the theme proceeds we become aware of a yet more thrilling tone—the unmuted solo violin is sustaining and swelling a long note above the orchestra. This leads to the solo continuation of the theme with leisurely breadth, until at last the full orchestra bursts in with a cadence-theme, which I quote mainly for the sake of rousing the reader's desire to hear a bold orchestral effect which the pianoforte cannot so much as indicate:

There is no means of representing on the pianoforte the strange and solemn effect of that bare octave for flutes and horns in the second bar. It recurs in due course in the recapitulation, just before the cadenza. This Adagio is full of beautiful points at every bar, and it is impossible to do justice to it in analysis. Further quotations are useless, but it may be well to call attention to the fine effect of the return of the first theme distributed in widely different octaves. The recapitulation is very regular, but the orchestral effects become fresh through the exigencies of transposition to the tonic, much as the lights and shadows in a building vary with the position of the sun.

BEETHOVEN

9. THIRTY-THREE VARIATIONS ON A WALTZ BY DIABELLI, FOR PIANOFORTE, OP. 120

(1900)

THIS, the greatest set of variations ever written, has a curious origin. In the winter of 1822–3, Diabelli, a successful music publisher and a deservedly popular writer of educational and otherwise useful music for the hour, invited all the composers then in Austria to join in a *Vaterländische Künstlerverein*, and each contribute a variation on a Waltz which he (Diabelli) provided as a theme. Fifty-one musicians accepted the invitation, and three names in the catalogue are of interest to us, namely, Beethoven, Schubert, and—Liszt! So that there are at the time of writing many not yet in the prime of life who have known the man who, as a *Wunderkind* of eleven, contributed with Beethoven and Schubert to Diabelli's *Vaterländische Künstlerverein*.

At the time of Diabelli's invitation Beethoven was fairly advanced in the work of sketching the Ninth Symphony; a fact which gives the greater significance to the extraordinary impulse that led him to throw off thus suddenly one of the three most enormous compositions ever written for a single instrument. Diabelli must have been somewhat astonished (to put it mildly) when, after long delay, Beethoven sent him—not the single variation he expected—but a huge volume, the publication of which Diabelli, with evident delight, announced in the following terms. 'We present here to the world Variations of no ordinary type, but a great and important masterpiece worthy to be ranked with the imperishable creations of the old Classics—such a work as only Beethoven, the greatest living representative of true art —only Beethoven, and no other, can produce. The most original structures and ideas, the boldest musical idioms and harmonies are here exhausted; every pianoforte effect based on a solid technique is employed, and this work is the more interesting from the fact that it is elicited from a theme which no one would otherwise have supposed capable of a working-out of that character in which our exalted Master stands alone among his contemporaries. The splendid Fugues, Nos. 24 and 32, will astonish all friends and connoisseurs of serious style, as will Nos. 6, 16, 17, 23, &c. the brilliant pianists; indeed all these variations, through the novelty of their ideas, care in working-out, and beauty in the most artful of their transitions, will entitle the work to a place beside Sebastian Bach's famous masterpiece in the same form.

124

We are proud to have given occasion for this composition, and have, moreover, taken all possible pains with regard to the printing to combine elegance with the utmost accuracy.'

This is surely one of the most intelligent publisher's puffs ever written. It was (almost unavoidably) perhaps a little indiscreet, from the contemporary point of view, to call the attention of 'connoisseurs of serious style' to the fugues; for Beethoven knew so much more about the 'serious style' than any one else then living, that in other fields he never seemed to his contemporaries to break half so many rules (or as they would have had it, to make half so many gross blunders) as in his contrapuntal movements. Most of the 'connoisseurs' of his day were probably too fully occupied in the enjoyment of a scandalizing discovery of two very obvious pairs of consecutive octaves in the fughetta, and some imperceptible consecutive fifths in the big fugue, to appreciate the new light these extraordinary movements threw on the possibilities of the 'serious style'. And the 'brilliant pianists' were probably more 'astonished' than gratified to find that the difficulties of the rapid variations were not made for the express purpose of redounding to the player's honour and glory, but were simply the outcome of ideas that had to be executed in the best practicable way, whether that way happened to be difficult or not.

Still, however much Diabelli's puff may have given the enemy cause to blaspheme, it was a most intelligent appreciation, speaking no less well for the culture of the musical public than for Diabelli's cleverness. It somewhat shakes one's complacency to imagine how a reference to the 'Goldberg' Variations would sound in a publisher's announcement of a modern novelty.

Diabelli expresses surprise that his theme should have made the basis for so extraordinary a work. If we look at it from the ordinary point of view, expecting fine sentiments and broad melody, we shall indeed find a difficulty in seeing anything in it. The utmost that can be said for it is that it is healthy, unaffected, and drily energetic. What, then, can have led Beethoven to write such a tremendous work on it?

Let us consider what means were hitherto in use in organizing variations. We have fully discussed the 'Goldberg' Variations, and have seen that in that work the variations were founded entirely on the bass, or the harmonies, or both. Another method in vogue in Bach's time, and very characteristically treated by Handel in well-known works, was to make the melody the sole support of the variations, as Bach himself once did in a pretty little *Aria Variata alla Maniera Italiana*. This method is suitable only for small and simple works. Then the melodic and harmonic treatments may be combined, with the results which we see in the more important variation movements in Mozart's mature chamber music and throughout all Beethoven's variations (except the present set), whether as movements in a sonata-work or as independent compositions. Probably Beethoven's Variations on a theme from *Prometheus*, op. 35, represent the largest result attainable by this combination of methods. Bach, in the 'Goldberg' Variations, by depriving himself of all resources that come from taking the melody of the theme as a guiding principle, gained a complete independence in melodic matter which enabled him to attain far more variety and expanse than would be possible in variations that depend as frequently on the melodic surface of the theme as on its harmonies. But whatever possibility there is of making modern variations on as large a scale as the 'Goldberg' Variations, that possibility must come in the shape of a theme which has other fundamental principles besides melody and harmony.

Now it is a remarkable achievement that Diabelli should have produced a theme which is equally rich in solid musical facts, from whatever point of view it is taken. I quote the first half in full:

Ex.1

The second half is on exactly the same lines bar for bar, the harmonies moving back again from dominant through subdominant to the tonic.

It may seem strange to devote a large space to the analysis of Diabelli's theme, but it is sufficient defence that to do so is to follow precisely what Beethoven does in the variations. It is actually more important to analyse the theme than to analyse the variations; for the theme contains the bare principles, while the variations embody these principles so clearly that if we grasp the principles, no wealth of complex detail can do otherwise than enhance our enjoyment and understanding of the whole, whereas the variations, apart from the theme and from each other, would not be intelligible. This, though it is their modern counterpart, is a work on very different lines from the 'Goldberg' Variations. The 'Goldberg' Variations need individual analysis, together with a careful observation of their very delicate and unobtrusive principles of grouping and contrasting. The present variations need no analysis beyond comparison with the theme; their grouping and contrasting explain themselves with dazzling effect, and their difficulties for us result mainly from our tendency to view music in a one-sided way as something in which rhythms, harmonies, and facts of structure are less real and important than the melodic surface which they support and render organic and expressive.

I propose not to attempt a description of this wonderful work variation by variation, but to take each element in the theme and briefly show its development in the variations. Beethoven's means of expression are not, like Bach's, remote from the art-forms of the present day, nor is there a tendency to take his work too lightly, as there most certainly is with Haydn and Mozart. Beethoven's later works are universally regarded as difficult, and the best method of analysis is that which will show that with all their wonderful depth and mystery they are actually more simple in principles than his earlier works, however crowded they may be with minute and curious detail.

Take, then, the melody of Diabelli's Waltz. Its main features are first the step—

(marked (b) in No. 1), with the corresponding step four bars later—

and secondly the rising sequences beginning at the ninth bar (marked (d)). Now some variations give the whole melody very recognizably, especially the first (*Alla Marcia, maestoso*), as is desirable at the beginning of a work of this form. Nothing can be more appropriate, after stating the naïve,. drily healthy theme, than an emphatic proof that this is to be a very grand and serious work, in the shape of something that resembles the melodic surface but is entirely solemn and grand in style:

Ex.2

After this Beethoven relapses into playing lightly with his theme. The initial melodic step is traceable in the extremely delicate second variation—

Ex.3

and, after a third variation of warmer and more contrapuntal character, in which it is a little less prominent—

Ex.4

but where the rhythm of (*d*) (see No. 1) begins to assert itself very strongly, it reappears as the principal idea in the next two variations:

Ex.5   Ex.6.

As the work proceeds, such melodic hints at the theme become less frequent and less necessary in view of the great range afforded by harmonic and rhythmic methods. The ninth variation, in the minor, is founded entirely on the initial turn (*a*):

Ex.7

The tenth, a most exciting whirlwind of sound, reproduces all the sequences and rhythms of the theme so clearly that it seems much more like a melodic variation than it really is; while in the eleventh the initial turn reappears again—

Ex.8

and is developed into something analogous in the twelfth:

Ex.9

The fifteenth variation gives the whole melodic outline so closely that its extraordinary freedom of harmony (the first half actually closes in the tonic) produces no effect of remoteness. The same applies to the large block of two variations, sixteen and seventeen, of which the sixteenth has the melody in the right hand—

Ex.10

and semiquavers in the left, while the seventeenth has the melody in the bass and the semiquavers above. These variations are so close to the surface of the theme that the amazingly distant keys touched on by their harmonies add only a sense of majesty and depth to the effect without producing complexity. This brings the first half of the work to a brilliant climax. Other important melodic identities are, Variation 20—

Ex.11

Imitated by right hand

one of the most awe-inspiring passages in music; the startling twenty-first variation with its changes from quick common to slower triple time whenever it reproduces the sequential passages marked (d) in the theme:

Ex.12

Then there is twenty-second, with the delightful transformation of figure (c) in the bass into an allusion to Mozart's 'Notte e giorno faticar'—the first number in *Don Giovanni*—

K

Ex.13

(Mozart's 'Notte e giorno faticar' has the accents reversed, thus—)

Ex.13a

and the twenty-third, with its orchestral brilliance and capricious rhythm—

Ex.14

and the fughetta, a wonderfully delicate and mysterious web of sounds on a figure suggested partly by the treble and partly by the bass of the first four bars of the theme:

Ex.15

Acting on a hint given him by the second half of Diabelli's theme, Beethoven inverts this in the second half of his fughetta:

Ex.15a

Then the next variation reproduces the opening of both halves quite simply—

Ex.16

though it is very free with the rest. As a reaction from the impressively thoughtful and calm fughetta it has an intensely humorous effect.

The next three variations are all structurally (though, as almost throughout the work, far from harmonically) identical with the theme; and the second of them, besides being a development of the preceding one, has the characteristic step (*b*) strongly marked in the bass:

Ex.17

(*b*)

After the twenty-eighth variation has brought this stage of the work to an exhilarating close, Beethoven follows Bach's example as shown at precisely the same stage (Variation 25) in the 'Goldberg' Variations, and boldly chooses the point at which we realize that the work is on a gigantic scale, as the point at which he shall enlarge our expectations of further developments more surprisingly than ever before. He gives us no less than three slow variations in the minor mode, producing an effect as weighty (even in proportion to the gigantic dimensions of the work) as that of a large slow movement in a sonata.

The second of these variations begins with a phrase in which the step (*b*) is embodied, perhaps rather by accident than by design—

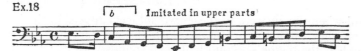

Ex.18   Imitated in upper parts

but in the second half (*d*) is clearly reproduced in most romantic passages—

Ex.19

a phrase so haunting that though Beethoven does not repeat the entire sections of this variation he marks the last four bars to be repeated.

The thirty-first variation is an extremely rich outpouring of highly ornamented melody, which to Beethoven's contemporaries must have been hardly intelligible, but which we, who have

learnt from Bach that a great artist's feeling is often more profound where his expression is most ornate, can recognize for one
of the most impassioned utterances in all music. The clearness
with which (a) and (b) of the theme are treated in the first two
bars (corresponding to the first eight of the theme):

Ex.20

prevents the greater freedom and elaboration of the continuation
from giving the hearer difficulty.

With the thirty-second variation the key changes to E♭, with
splendid effect in feeling of freedom and enlarged activity. The
structure of the theme is abandoned, and the movement is
worked out freely as a large double fugue. But no loss of connexion is felt, for the two subjects which are announced in
combination at the outset neatly epitomize the first part of
Diabelli's Waltz, omitting bars 5–8 (as being melodically mere
sequential repetition of bars 1–4), but giving (b), (d), and the
cadence on the dominant unmistakably:

Ex.21

(d) in descending sequence

And when the answers to these two subjects appear in the lower
parts they seem to correspond with the six bars here quoted,
much as the theme's second half corresponds with its first. This
done, the fugue is worked out on a large scale. The two subjects
are eventually treated by inversion:

Ex.22

also in stretto (i.e., the answer overlapping the subject); until a
climax is reached, with a pause. Then a new version of the first
subject is discussed in combination with a third subject (derived
from (x) of No. 21 by inverted diminution), thus:

Ex.23

The pianissimo tone and running motion contrast sharply with the preceding treatment and style: but soon the old version of the fugue themes bursts in fortissimo, much increased in impetuosity by combination with the new running figure. Suddenly there is a grandly dramatic pause. The storm of sound melts away, and, through one of the most ethereal and—I am amply justified in saying—appallingly impressive passages ever written, we pass quietly to the last variation. It is a return to the melody of the theme, but a transfigured melody, in which no trace of things unspiritual is left:

Ex 24

It is profoundly characteristic of the way in which (as Diabelli himself seems partly to have grasped) this work develops and enlarges the great aesthetic principles of balance and climax embodied in the 'Goldberg' Variations, that it ends quietly. The freedom necessary for an ordinary climax on modern lines was secured already in the great fugue, placed, as it was, in a foreign key; and now Beethoven, like Bach, rounds off his work by a peaceful return home—a home that seems far removed from those stormy experiences through which alone such ethereal calm can be attained.

The short but sublime coda contains a suggestion for a thirty-fourth variation, in the passage beginning—

Ex.25

and concludes by taking the initial figure—

and working it up by increasingly elaborate ornamentations into a running passage which swells out and dies mysteriously away, till a single forte chord reveals that the work is over.

In this short sketch I have dwelt on the melodic threads, as they are what is most difficult to grasp in listening to this work, while at the same time they reveal more immediately than other points the essential simplicity that underlies Beethoven's infinite wealth of minute detail. For those who wish farther to follow the structure of the work, I subjoin a tabular sketch of the rhythmic and tonal framework of the theme, with a list of variations that illustrate the points suggested:

First half.—Four bars tonic chord; 4 bars dominant; 2 and 2 bars rising sequences; 4 separate bars forming cadence in dominant.

Second half.—Rhythmic scheme the same as in first half, the harmonies moving back again from dominant through subdominant to tonic.

With so sharply articulated a framework Beethoven has an entirely free hand with his harmonies, and there is not one variation that does not alter them in very striking and infinitely various ways. Thus, in the first eight bars the supertonic may be substituted for the dominant, with wonderful effect, as in Variation 8, at *—

Ex.26

or the flat supertonic, as in Variation 30, where the whole variation, except its first and last phrases, is practically in D flat. Similarly the first half may close in another key than the dominant, as E minor (Variations 5, 14), A minor (25), A flat (30), or even the tonic (15). And in the first eight bars the *alternation* of chords, apart from their harmonic identity, may be done on less simple plans, as in Variations 3, 4, 5, and 29.

On the other hand, the rhythmic framework is seldom much disguised; to trace it is highly stimulating to one's sense of form, a faculty too much neglected in recent times. The only variations in which the rhythm is at all disguised are Nos. 4, 11, and 12, in which a bar is capriciously omitted from one of the 4-bar groups; 21, where the alternate 8-bar groups are in different times; 23, where a bar is omitted at the first cadence; 24, where the fugue-form aims at a more fluid and less formally rhythmic style; 29, where each half is epitomized in six bars; 31, where in each half the first 4-bar groups are represented by one each, while the rest expands as it proceeds, until at the cadences it overflows its own bars (there are twelve instead of nine quavers in the last bars of each part, a fact Beethoven does not show by a time-signature); the fugue, where the form of the theme is quite abandoned; and the last variation where the 4-bar groups are compressed into two bars, while the rest answers bar for bar to the theme. Of these nine cases of rhythmic alteration only four, viz., the fughetta, Nos. 29, 31, and the fugue, are of great importance; and this is not a large proportion out of 33.

Lastly, we must not forget Variation 13, which is a most humorous representation of the rhythmic skeleton and nothing more; except for harmonies that take care of themselves.

10. SONATA IN A MAJOR, OP. 47 FOR VIOLIN AND PIANOFORTE, (DEDICATED TO KREUTZER)

(1900)

$\left\{ \begin{array}{l} Adagio\ sostenuto,\ \text{A major, 3/4, leading to—} \\ Presto,\ \text{A minor, C.} \end{array} \right.$
Andante con Variazioni, F major, 2/4.
FINALE.—Presto, A major, 6/8.

So popular a classic as the 'Kreutzer' Sonata needs either no analysis or else a very detailed one. It is not, like the Schumann Quintet, a work in which certain minute points can be made to throw light on some special peculiarity of artistic method, for it is thoroughly in touch with the early classical conceptions.

For the present it must suffice to mention a few respects in which the 'Kreutzer' Sonata is more unusual than disproportionate familiarity disposes us to recognize.

The first of such points that occurs to me is that it was, and still is, a very unusual thing that a work introduced so broadly in a major key should proceed to a stormy and passionate first movement in the minor. I am aware of only two instances before the 'Kreutzer' Sonata, the first being Mozart's G major Violin Sonata (K. 379), where, however, the opening adagio is felt as something much more independent than an introduction, and the second being a very early pianoforte quartet on precisely the same lines as the Mozart sonata, by Beethoven himself—a work which he afterwards carefully disowned.

It is, again, perhaps interesting from a dramatic point of view to note that in the introduction to the 'Kreutzer' Sonata it is only the first four bars (for the unsupported violin) that are really in A major, though their breadth is such that the seal of A major seems at once set upon the work. But the entry of the pianoforte casts a most dramatic cloud over the opening and sets the tone for that wonderfully wistful, yet terse anticipatory expression that makes this introduction one of the landmarks in musical history.

As to the following presto it is, perhaps, well to guard oneself against a misconception that has misled not only a certain great novelist but also many less nervous music-lovers into underrating the rest of the work. The mood of the first movement is very fiery and passionate, but it is the passion of Homeric fighting, not that of Aeschylean tragedy: and the rich set of ornate variations follows with exactly the right contrast of tone; while the happy and witty finale (though originally intended for a smaller and earlier work, which it would most certainly have overbalanced) is the one possible outcome of the other two movements that is neither trivial nor sententious.

No doubt the first movement is the finest. But the principle that the end is the only true place for the finest part of a work of art may be popular and may seem obvious, but it is very far from being correct. Whether a work of art passes before one through time, as in music and literature, or stands in space as in painting and sculpture, the true place of its finest features depends on logic and proportion, be the result what it may.

SCHUBERT

11. BLUMENBALLADE: 'VIOLA'

(1900)

As a rule, songs are easier to understand when they are not analysed; but when a song is expanded to nearly the dimensions of an important sonata, there is some call for a little comment that may prepare the listener's mind for so large a work.

'Viola' is not the longest of Schubert's songs, though it is by far the most perfect and beautiful of the long ones, and stands among his ripest works. It was written in March 1823, when he was twenty-six years old and was about to begin the composition of *Fierrabras*, his largest opera. Five months previously, he had written the two movements of his most flawless and profound orchestral work, the 'Unfinished' Symphony, and had revised his huge Mass in A flat. He was soon about to begin on the great song-cycle, *Die schöne Müllerin*, and before the year was out he finished it and wrote the incidental music to *Rosamunde*, besides several of his most exquisite single songs, such as 'Auf dem Wasser zu singen', 'Du bist die Ruh', and 'Dass sie hier gewesen'. Among these 'Viola' is well worthy of its position. Its superiority to the other very long songs is not altogether accounted for by its later date; for though 'Der Taucher' and 'Die Einsamkeit', to take only two instances, were written when Schubert was eighteen, yet he was then capable of the 'Erlkönig' and 'Gretchen am Spinnrade', two of the most masterly and powerful dramatic creations in the whole literature of song.

Strange to say, outside Schubert's own genius the main circumstance that was conducive to the perfection of 'Viola' lay in the words. Composers have a habit of seizing on the great things a poem might mean, before they have time to reason out coldly what it actually does mean. In the case of a great composer this habit has the most splendid results in the setting of great poetry, for the ideas of such poetry flash into the composer's mind and translate themselves into his own forms and language with the most spirited accuracy and sureness of touch. It would be extremely difficult to find any important instance of a great composer's setting of a great poem where the composer could be proved to have missed the point of the words. On the other hand this quick sympathy is not conducive to an equally quick discriminating faculty. A composer will see that the sentiments, contrasts, and proportions of a poem will easily run parallel with those of a beautiful musical design, long before he realizes that

137

the sentiment of the poem is unreal and its style affected. The unreal sentiment is to him so much raw material for translation into substantial deep-felt art, and the affected style a hint for the happy use of spontaneous characterization in harmony and rhythm. Poetry that is capable of musical setting at all is to the great composer so much raw material for a musical work of art, very raw if it be feeble poetry, and overmastering in its inspiring effect if it be great in itself.

The words of 'Viola' are by no means great, but they naturally elicit a very effective musical structure; and the unreality of their sentiment is translated by Schubert into something unrealistic indeed, but not unreal. 'Der Taucher', by Schiller, was a far finer poem, but Schubert could not bring out from it a strong appeal to one's sense of musical form; and the necessity for doing justice to it as a dramatic piece of declamation prevented Schubert from bringing out its most convincing formal element as poetry—its rolling ballad-rhythm. 'Viola' is by Schober, a man whose sole claim to consideration is that he was a good friend to Schubert, and wrote verses into which Schubert could read both poetry and form when he set them to music. The rhythm of 'Viola' is not so swinging as to be lost in slow declamation, nor the style so declamatory as to suggest breaking up the rhythm.

'Viola' begins with a long refrain, a call to the snowdrop (or, as the Germans call it, the 'snowbell') to 'ring its bell in the meads', as herald of Spring, the bridegroom, returning victorious from his fight with Winter. Schubert sets this to the following melody, prefacing it with a pianoforte introduction, which gives the same theme in a simpler form. (One would not have thought a simpler form possible or effective if the main version were all one knew, but with Schubert both are in the highest degree poetical and alive.)

Ex.1   Mässig

The pianoforte then begins a new figure:

Ex.2

which furnishes a suggestive accompaniment to the account of Spring's victorious return. The snowdrop is bidden to summon all the flowers to greet 'Spring, the bridegroom'; the music, following the festive character of the words, modulates brightly to the dominant, where, after a formal close, the pianoforte has a short interlude, in which Ex. 2 (*b*) is given a clear thematic character:

Ex.3

Then the snowdrop is invoked again to 'ring the flowers up from their sleep', which naturally brings about the return of Ex. 1 *in extenso*, with the added accompaniment, in monotone, of the rhythm that was used for 'victorious Spring':

Thus the first main section of the work is rounded off in firm musical form and yet with accurate following of the words.

A deliberate change to a rather distant key is now made; and an altogether new movement in quick triple time with a rippling accompaniment sets out in F major. 'Viola', the violet, is the first to hear the thrilling sound:

Ex.4

Du Vi - o - la, zar - tes
Kind, hörst zu-erst den Won-ne - laut

She hurries to meet the bridegroom, and does not stop to see whether others are as forward. Suddenly she is alarmed (the pianoforte rhythm becomes syncopated, and distant modulations start from a sudden plunge into the minor):

Ex. 5

fp   &c.
Doch ein   ängst-lich-es   Ge - fühl
&c.

Slowly the bass descends chromatically from F, and thus, in a fine series of distant but sequential modulations, and an accompaniment that follows the vacillations of Viola and the situation with perfect faithfulness and musical spontaneity, Schubert brings us to the extremely distant key, G minor. The tempo becomes very slow as the violet pauses at finding herself alone without signs of sisters or bridegroom. Then, stricken with shame, she flies hither and thither, far and wide, looking everywhere for signs of life and companionship in the grass and hedges. Rapid modulations, always sequential and broad, and quick common time with a tremolo in semiquavers, here, as always, faithfully follow the words while retaining full control over musical structure. As the violet becomes wearied and despondent the accompaniment subsides and becomes a monotonous quaver figure in A flat, the original key—

Ex.6

and on this Ex. 1 returns again—an invocation to the snowdrop to summon the other flowers to the aid of Viola.

With superb structural and tonal power, Schubert puts his next movement in the same key—thus laying due stress on the tonic after all these wanderings, and at the same time expressing a fine contrast between the confidence of the flowers, which now arrive in procession, and the bewildered shame of the lost Viola. Also the effect of an utter change of rhythm and matter without any change of key is in itself unusual and bold.

Here is the new theme, spaciously started after five bars of broad symphony:

Ex.7

So when Spring arrives (which he does to the tune of Ex. 3— one of the most splendid strokes of musical structure in the whole range of song) he finds all the flowers there to meet him, except his favourite—Viola. He sends them all in search of her —a breathless rapid movement, beginning in B natural major (a new and somewhat remote key), fitly characterizes this search:

Ex.8

(From here to the end the sequence of keys is, but for a momentary break at Viola's death, one of rising thirds, viz., A flat to (C flat) B natural, B natural to D, D minor to F, and thence, through a touch of D, to A flat.) They reach the spot where Viola is wasting away in solitude and shame, but they reach it too late; the delicate flower, its love and longing too great for its strength, has perished:

Ex.9

Doch es sitzt, das lie - be Kind stumm und bleich, das Haupt ge-blickt,

It will be seen that the key, F major, is that in which Viola first appeared (Ex. 4). Schubert, as he announces the death, passes into D minor, the one key more distant than that G minor in which we had Viola's discovery that she was alone. From this extreme point, D minor, a very fine 'enharmonic modulation'— (a change of meaning in an equivocal chord):

Ex.10

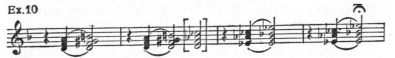

leads back to the tonic, A flat, where the song is perfectly rounded off by a final return to Ex. 1, unvaried, as the snowdrop is bidden to toll Viola's knell.

SCHUMANN

12. NOVELLETTE IN F SHARP MINOR, OP. 21, NO. 8, FOR PIANOFORTE

(1900)

IN Schumann's pianoforte works, small or large, we have not to deal with the complex organizations of classical sonata forms; our task is rather that generally hopeless one of the man who tries to analyse songs. Schumann's pianoforte lyrics depend, not on elaborate structure and wide resource in the transformation of themes and variety in length of phrases, but on the simple and effective alternation and contrast of vividly characteristic self-contained musical strophes. The true aesthetic analysis of a *Novellette* or *Phantasiestück* of Schumann would mean an analysis of the function and balance of practically every note in each section; and such an analysis would be not only tedious in the extreme, but hideously difficult to understand, and the universal love—almost personal in its quality—that is felt for Schumann's works shows it to be ludicrously unnecessary and pointless.

It is, however, well that the reader should bear in mind that while the large formal analysis of a work of Schumann's reveals nothing but the most coarse-grained and obvious organization, there really is this extremely minute and perfect organization behind it and maintained by it. Signs are not wanting at the present day of a tendency (among critics of the type that knows no history) to revive the exploded charge against Schumann that his sequences are childishly obvious, his form amateurish, &c., &c. All this is just as elementary as the objections one can imagine that a well-read ancient Greek or Roman would make to the jingling effect of rhyme in poetry.

Schumann's instrumental lyrics contain some of the finest and most highly organized texture to be found in any art. This texture was made possible by the work of Haydn, Mozart, and Beethoven in the direction of reconciling the epigrammatic and rich texture of Bach and Handel with the necessary broad and open devices of modern form. Beethoven had already produced some genuine and exquisite lyrics in his *Bagatelles*; and Schumann found polyphony and form so thoroughly reconciled that (aiding and stimulating himself by studying that greatest and most romantic of pre-formal polyphonists, Bach) he soon became the greatest of instrumental lyric poets. From short lyrics, like 'Warum?' it is an easy and absolutely legitimate step to large agglomerations of lyric organisms, such as the *Novel-*

lettes, or the great *Humoreske*; and we have listened to Beethoven's Sonata, *Les Adieux*, in vain if we cannot realize that Schumann's extra-musical titles—consisting, as they do, so entirely of matters of feeling and character[1]—in no way militate against the pure artistic value of the works under them. Not even against *Carnaval* (about which Schumann himself had his doubts) can anything cogent be said on this score.

To turn to the matter in hand—the eighth *Novellette* begins passionately in F sharp minor with a large 4-bar theme on a seething triplet accompaniment of which the bass rises steadily:

Ex.1

This is passed through alto, treble, tenor, and bass, alternately in tonic and dominant, like a very loose and simple fugue. A contrasting theme in A major (still, like the whole first section, accompanied in rushing triplets) follows, and leads back to F sharp where Ex. 1 returns in canon, thus:

Ex.2

After fresh stormy sequences, the first section works to a climax with the theme, first in the bass, then in the treble, in the subdominant (B minor, with very fine effect), at last breaking off the triplets and concluding with the following cadence from a rapid and bold sequence of remote harmonies:

Ex. 3

---

[1] e.g., 'Warum,' 'Grillen,' &c. Even when his allusions are literary, they are allusions to the literature of character and feeling (e.g., 'Kreisleriana', the works of Jean Paul Richter, &c.), not to the literature of incident and plot.

The effect of the final unison after those rich harmonies is very grand.

Schumann now continues as if he were going to work out a great scherzo with two trios. The first trio is in the dominant major (D flat = C sharp)—

Ex. 4

and with its lighter rhythm and delicate playfulness—tinged in the second part with a more caressing, drooping tone—forms a sharp contrast to the first section. It sounds like the entry of some light-hearted, gentle character, to whom *Sturm und Drang* is a mystery, and so, when it seems to ask what *Sturm und Drang* means—

Ex. 5

it breaks off and the first section returns more sternly and stormily than ever. The A major subsidiary is omitted, and instead we have in the tonic a new canonic derivative of the main theme:

Ex. 6

This leads to the last lines of the section, which are reproduced as at first, and are all the finer in this fresh and bolder context.

The second trio follows in D major, an unmistakable hunting-chorus. The solution of the *Sturm und Drang* is now to be sought in the open air, and in manly energy and strength:

Ex. 7

This is carried on with immense vigour on a large scale, till gradually it dies away as if in the distance:

Ex.8

The bass keeps up the figure

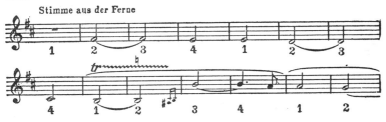

throughout the wonderful passage that now follows as if to put an end for ever to the prospect of a return to the early *Sturm und Drang*. Over the dying hunting rhythm of the bass steals a slow, soft melody—a 'voice from afar' (*Stimme aus der Ferne*) Schumann calls it:

Ex.9

Stimme aus der Ferne

(As the rhythm of a slow phrase across a quick tempo is not always easy to read rightly, I number the bars in four according to their rhythmic swing.)

When this has come to a close, Schumann makes a pause. The scheme of writing a great scherzo with two trios, strongly as it impresses itself on the listener's expectation (whether he is, or is not, sufficiently a musical expert to know it)—this scheme is no longer adequate. Whoever the hero may be—whether Schumann himself, or Schumann's general conception of the artist—

L

whoever the hero may be whose period of *Sturm und Drang* we may (for convenience in analysis) suppose Schumann to represent in the first section, he has now had a glimpse of some ideal that makes a return to his former condition impossible.

The ensuing short movement—headed by Schumann *Fortsetzung* ('Continuation') is a slow and dream-like working-out of the theme given by the *Stimme aus der Ferne*, on a slowly rising bass and in very free meditative rhythm. It closes in a repetition of the passage Ex. 8 where the hunting rhythm dies away in the bass; and it appends these solemn final chords:

Ex.10

Adagio

What good is a beautiful dream to us if we do not awaken from it the better able to bear our part in the active world? and what truth is there in ideals which only make the world we live in seem false and distasteful?

The practice of drawing morals from works of art is generally objectionable and futile, but in this case the moral is itself an artistic one, and can hardly be denied as a true, though imperfect and threadbare, inference from the tone and structure of Schumann's present finale, entitled by him *Fortsetzung und Schluss*— 'Continuation and End'.[1] If we were asked what further developments were possible at this point, we could never find any better answer than 'a great contrast; vigorous new material—not a return to the opening, for that mood has been lost beyond recovery—but a new organization with some slight immediate connexion with the preceding passage, but far greater contrast; working in, if possible, a transformation of the *Stimme aus der Ferne* theme later on'. Supposing, for sheer amusement's sake, that we could have guessed all this, it would still remain to be seen whether any one but Schumann could have made sense of it. Let us see how he works it out.

He takes the two solemn last chords of Ex. 10 (an exact compromise between the 'authentic' and the ecclesiastical 'plagal' cadence) and makes them the main feature in a very vigorous theme, beginning a new movement in D major:—

[1] I venture to use it as a half-figurative means of analysing the work; not because I believe the work to be 'programme music', but because a more purely aesthetic explanation would be extremely difficult to follow, and would not give a much more accurate idea than the present very general and abstract figure.

Ex.11

The character of this whole movement, with its strong harmony, rising sequences, and square 8-bar phrases, is eminently that of a man who carries his ideals with him into a vigorous practical and social life.

Schumann works out the above (Ex. 11) as a 'ternary' melody (i.e., one that, if we designate themes by letters, may be described by the formula A, B, A), constructing his first and third phrases so that they end as well as begin on those two solemn chords that are now to form the motto for the rest of the work.

Now we begin to see prospects of a new and larger scherzo with two trios. The first trio is a graceful and epigrammatic ternary melody in A major (the dominant)—

Ex 12

very characteristically and richly harmonized. When it reaches its end, the skip from its dominant chord to the first chord of Ex. 11 (which returns *notatim*) is extremely bold and surprising.

All this time the impression of a thorough and noble enjoyment of a manly life is heightened and rendered humorous by the fact that the tempo becomes faster and faster as the movement proceeds. By the time we reach the second trio this increase has become considerable. The second trio begins with another large 'binary' melody, in the rich and dark key[1] of B flat. It is well worth the listener's while to note the fourteen steps of chromatic scale in its bass—a great element in its broad aspiring effect. I quote overleaf only the treble and bass. The inner parts are half polyphonic and half purely harmonic:—

[1] The reader must not imagine that these epithets are based on fanciful notions about the character of keys. In themselves, keys have no character; but in relation to one another their characters become very pronounced and quite fixed. E.g., B flat to D (the present example) is a dark and warm tonal colour, as shown by the universal practice of great composers. Compare the very same *relationship* (though not the same *keys*) in Beethoven, slow movement of op. 7 (A flat to C), second subject of B flat Quartet op. 130 (G flat to B flat), &c., &c.

Ex.13

The continuation is of the like surging nature, but in still darker harmonic colouring, and ends in a repetition of the above, modified so as to close in its tonic, B flat.

Now Schumann has a mind to develop this second trio further. So he begins a new theme in D minor, forte—

Ex.14

also on a chromatically rising foundation, and with a fresh increase of pace. The gay and capricious sequel in A minor—

Ex.15

&c.

becomes important. Its second figure, here marked (*x*), is treated in chromatically descending sequence:

Ex.16

This, repeated in lower octaves, begins to lose its gaiety as it becomes developed low in the bass. The development becomes restless and strangely dark, a great crescendo arises, the continual quickening of time (now no longer a sign of exhilaration) brings matters to a crisis in which the great theme of the *Stimme aus der Ferne* bursts forth in D minor and F major, grandly and sternly this time, till, with a softer turn of harmony, it suddenly melts in a beautiful phrase (marked by Schumann with that untranslatable word *Innig*[1]), and gently leads back, not to any sentimental process that would ruin the whole design and feeling, but simply to the gay A minor group of themes, Exx. 15 and 16. The ideals have prevailed in active life once more. From the continuation of Ex. 16 Schumann this time finds his way back easily to B flat and Ex. 13, the whole of which he repeats. From thence the obvious course is 'Scherzo da capo e fine': i.e., repeat the main theme Ex. 11 *in extenso*, slackening and emphasizing the last chords so as to end the noble work worthily with its own noble motto:

Ex 17

13. QUINTET IN E FLAT MAJOR, OP. 44, FOR PIANOFORTE, TWO VIOLINS, VIOLA, AND VIOLONCELLO

(1900)

Allegro brillante. E flat major, ¢.
In Modo d'una Marcia. Poco largamente, C minor, ¢
SCHERZO. *Molto vivace.* E flat major, 6/8.
Allegro ma non troppo. E flat major, ¢.

WITH a work so popular as Schumann's Quintet, the only useful kind of analysis (beyond the quotation of themes) is such as may help to revive in our minds an appreciation of those points which familiarity causes us to miss.

Of such points the first movement contains one which illustrates the keystone of Schumann's art in the construction of large non-lyric instrumental works. The first theme:

Ex.1

attracts so much attention by the wide, sturdy strides of its first

---

[1] 'From the heart' would be a bad, conventional, and sentimental version, but might serve to give to one who knew no German a notion of the force of the word, though not of its simplicity and delicacy.

figure (*a*), and emphasizes it so constantly in the sequel and derivatives—

Ex.2

that it is impossible for the violoncello to throw in a casual leap of an octave in minims without implying the first theme; as, for example, in the prelude to the beautiful long-drawn dialogue of the second subject:

Ex 3

Now the significance of this kind of point is not merely that Schumann is a delightfully epigrammatic composer with a great power of making very simple things tell; for these are simply the qualities of all great artists. The more peculiar importance of the point just quoted lies in its bearing on Schumann's special methods as an artist of the 'romantic' rather than the classical school. He is writing an altogether new type of sonata-work; a kind that stands to the classical sonata somewhat as a very beautiful and elaborate mosaic stands to a landscape-picture. In the mosaic the material and structure necessitate and render appropriate an otherwise unusual simplicity and hardness of outline and treatment, while at the same time making it desirable that the subjects should be such that this simple treatment may easily lend them subtlety of meaning—just as, on the other hand, the costly stones of which the mosaic is made have in themselves many an exquisite gradation of shade and tone, though the larger contrasts and colours of the work as a connected whole are far more simple and obvious than those of a painting. In the At the present time, when a growing interest in the highest types of musical organization tends to make our more abstruse-minded enthusiasts somewhat impatient of what does not exercise all their faculties at once, it is as well to bear these things in mind. No better opportunity could be found for re-awakening in ourselves an appreciation of Schumann's artistic power and acumen than by specially listening to the strings next time we hear the Quintet. Schumann writes for these solo strings even more simply than for the orchestral strings in his concertos, a fact that would be inconceivable in chamber music on classical lines: yet every note tells, and the instruments are vividly characterized in spite of the preponderance of the pianoforte throughout, because all this simplicity of texture is in exact keeping with the splendidly motived rigidity of sequence and exactness of repetition.

In the development two points should be specially noted; first, its episodic introduction (the fact that it is episodic is of subtle effect in relation to the mosaic-like structure of the whole, apart from its powerful dramatic use later on):

Ex.4

and, secondly, the way in which the strings accompany the pianoforte throughout its long passage on (*b*) diminished, with suggestions of (*a*):

Ex.5

Note also that though the second half of the development repeats the first half a tone lower, yet the beginning and end of the repeat are changed. There is room for freedom even in mosaics, and this is just the kind of freedom that tells.

The slow movement and scherzo need no quotation. It is, however, worth while applying to them the principles I have here attempted to illustrate; and particular attention should be paid to the fine, sombre passage before the second episode, where the episodic introduction to the development of the first movement (No. 4) is given with most dramatic gloom. Also it sometimes escapes notice that the theme of the second episode is derived from the principal theme (see over):—

Ex.6

Furthermore, it should be borne in mind that in classical works the formal outlines tend to become more obvious as the work proceeds. Hence, as Schumann's instrumental works proceed, they become less and less radically different from the corresponding things in older classics, since their rigid outlines become more and more appropriate from the classical as well as the 'romantic' points of view.

Thus, after a scherzo (from which it is needless to quote) that might almost come from Beethoven as far as eboration and rhythms are concerned, except for the uniformly massive treatment of the strings, we come to a finale which crowns the noble structure with untarnished classical power and yet is in perfect keeping with the 'romanticism' of the rest, if indeed it does not actually enhance and develop it. What makes the finale so especially classical is the freedom of its form; for free forms need unusually clear and rigid exposition, not because the hearer is unaccustomed to them, but because, as their very rarity implies, they are the results of subtle and difficult qualities in the rest of the artistic scheme.

For instance, there are many subtleties and surprises, needing specially clear treatment, in the effect of a movement of which the first theme begins in a foreign key, as does Schumann's present finale with its emphatic opening on the subdominant of G minor (not C minor, as is sometimes stated).

Ex.8

Beethoven himself in such a case is hardly less sectional than Schumann, so strong is the necessity for doing the utmost that can be done by emphasis, rhythm, and repetition to make the real tonality clear. The formal nucleus of the present finale is a very concise and free binary organism, i.e., first subject in G minor and E flat (the real tonic), second subject in G major— a

Ex. 9

Ex.10

development (very short, free, and episodic) in B natural major—

Ex.11

and E major:

Ex.12

leading to a recapitulation of the first subject displaced through
a wide range of changing keys, so devised as to bring round the
second subject in the tonic.

The coda which follows is almost as long as the whole of the
movement so far. This is not so very unusual; precisely the
same may be said of the finales of Beethoven's Quartets in
C major and C sharp minor, and of his Eighth Symphony and
G major Concerto. And there is no lack of balance or feeling
of redundance when the coda contains such a startling impulse
for fresh development as is given by the entry of the opening

theme of the first movement at what seems at first to be the approaching end.

Here are the premonitions of that entry; they are worth quoting, as they are not always noticed. (They occur after Ex. 8 has been treated in brilliant fugue, and Ex. 12 has been grandly brought into the tonic.)

Ex.13

And here is the combination of the augmented first movement theme in double fugue with the finale theme:

Ex.14

It is very significant that almost the whole of the large fugue-passage that follows is in three-part writing, a fact that gives it much of its extraordinary openness and weight. Really, if one were not so apt to forget it, powerful three-part writing is a considerable *tour de force*, and its use here is one of the many points in which very popular classics turn out more highly organized than we always remember them to be.

After this fugue Schumann gathers up the earlier threads of his coda and crowns this, his best known work, with an impression of superb formal balance and finality.

CHOPIN

(1900)

ÉTUDES.—C sharp minor, op. 25, No. 7.
D flat major (for the *Méthode des Méthodes*), No. 3.
F minor (ditto), No. 1.
C minor, op. 25, No. 12.

CHOPIN'S Études stand alone. With the single exception of
Brahms in his Variations on a theme of Paganini, no other composer has so nobly overcome the immense difficulty of writing
works that shall systematize and exhibit, one by one, the extreme
resources of the modern pianoforte, while all the time remaining
spontaneous art of a high order. Before Chopin, the only great
composer who had done this for any instrument was Bach, who,
with characteristic modesty and simplicity, embraced an enormous mass of his grandest keyboard works under the general
title of *Clavierübung*. Here, it is true, he was only translating the
French and English custom of calling suites 'Lessons'. For
Bach the problem was not what it was for Chopin. The resources
of Bach's keyed instruments (harpsichord, clavichord, and organ)
were at once simpler and less easy to specialize than those of the
modern pianoforte, and in order to exhibit them all as clearly as
possible Bach had only to write freely in the largest forms his art
could devise. Hence, in his *Clavierübung*—comprising, as it does,
the 'Inventions and Symphonies', the six great Partitas, the
monumental Thirty Variations (with only one exception the
greatest set of variations ever written), the great E flat Prelude
and Fugue for organ, a collection of some of his most elaborate
Chorale Preludes (including 'The Giant'), the Four Duets, the
'Italian' Concerto, and the French Overture—in all this vast collection there can never arise any question of a conflict between
instrumental technique and artistic value—a point made all
the more clear by his choice of title. No one but Bach himself
could have been either so modest or so familiar with the
grandeur of these works as to think of them in the prosaic
aspect of *Clavierübung*.

With the development of the pianoforte the problem of Étude-
writing took a formidable shape; and no great composer systematically attempted an artistic solution of it from the death of
Bach until Chopin grappled with it and won a grand victory.
Mozart, it is true, wrote pianoforte sonatas for his pupils (some
of which he himself noted in his own catalogue of his works as

'*für einen Anfänger*'), but, for one thing, they were sonatas first and Études only in a very remote secondary way, and for another thing most of them fall within a single period of three years during which his best energies were engaged in dramatic works such as *Thamos*, and those two colossal operas, *Idomeneo* and *Die Entführung* Chopin was the first and has so far remained the only great artist who put a true poet's best work into compositions that are specifically Études, not compositions essentially in some independent large classical form and incidentally called Études because they happen to present clear types of instrumental difficulties. Beethoven's knowledge of the pianoforte was unfathomable, but he wrote no Études, though his sketch-books contain many 'exercises' (*Übungen*—mechanical formulas of instrumental difficulties—to be carefully distinguished from *Studien* or Études—works of art founded on types of instrumental difficulties), and he took a deep and critical interest in the works of Czerny and Cramer. Schumann, again, calls his grandest set of variations *Études Symphoniques*, and the variation-form is exceedingly favourable to the exposition of typical instrumental resources; but here also the work is variations first and Études afterwards. Schumann's remaining work in this field is his two delightful collections of transcriptions from Paganini's Violin Caprices.

Since Chopin, the only great writer of *Studien* is Brahms, and his noble Variations on a theme of Paganini are again variations first and *Studien* afterwards; while, as with Schumann, his remaining *Studien* consist of extraordinary transcriptions of other composers' works. On the other hand, he has left an astonishing collection of *Übungen*—fifty-one formulas carried mechanically straight up and down the keyboard, and covering almost the whole of modern technique, with much of the technique of the future. Perhaps this work indicates that in Brahms's view hardly anything is possible between pure formula and such independent art as that of the Variations on a theme of Paganini. Certain it is that Chopin's Études are the only extant great works of art that really owe their character to their being Études. As to the indefatigable Czerny and Cramer, the former has certainly impaired the value of his excellent formulas by embedding them in teaspoonfuls of inferior musical jam,[1] just as the latter has sometimes impaired his by his vehicle of wholesome, but dry, musical sponge-cake. For in free music instrumental formulas do not obligingly put themselves into all their possible positions successively, and the attempt to force such formulas into an ordi-

---

[1] At the same time, when excellent authorities tell me that Czerny's work is no longer of any educational value, I don't believe them.

nary musical mould generally means the sacrifice of their less usual and more difficult positions, for which the gain of so much inferior music is a very poor compensation. Even that venerable and truly inventive writer, Moscheles, has hardly produced such musical Études as can claim to be more than 'the greatest of all but the great'.

With Chopin the case is otherwise. His wide range of harmony, and his wayward uses of it, cause his 'figures' to assume fairly well any position that is humanly possible;[1] while, on the other hand, as if to squeeze from his brain the uttermost particle of resource that shall be as artistic as it is technically valuable, he shows a marked preference for such types of instrumental treatment as are difficult rather for sheer sustained effort, or for gradation of touch or tone, than for any particular knack that needs putting through set positions.

Before proceeding to comment on the four Études selected for the present programme, I must pause to answer the reader's inevitable question why I have not mentioned Liszt. I trust that an honest answer will offend no one, when I freely confess that, with a few exceptions, Liszt's Études seem to me to depend so much on the charm of his own splendid and noble personality that for others to play them always suggests the parable of the giant's robe. For the most part, regarded purely as compositions, their limits in thematic invention, as well as in all harmonic resources except such as are otiose, make it all but impossible for any one who has not in some way come under the magnetic and inspiring influence of their author's personality to do his memory justice. For the very same reason that I would give ten years' experience to have heard Liszt himself play them, I feel a great repugnance when those quasi-extempore fantasias that once flowed from the venerable Abbé's hands, to fall on his rapt audience like some affectionate half-secular blessing, are now turned to account for the base glorification of every brilliant player's agility. It is the giant's robe without the giant. With Chopin we need have no fear; in his Études we always find the giant in the robe, be the player who he may.

The four here grouped form a scheme of musical contrasts rather than an illustration of such a dry subject as instrumental technique. Less dry, however, is the matter with which we started, viz., the reconciliation of technique with art. Intimately connected with this is an aspect of Chopin very remote from that of the 'elegant salon-writer' still commonly held; the aspect of

---

[1] In this connexion, Moscheles's first opinion of Chopin's Études is quaintly significant. In 1833 he wrote of them: 'My thoughts, and consequently my fingers, ever stumble and sprawl at certain crude modulations.'

him as a hard-headed student of classical music—a musical
scholar whose work in certain directions may be no less fitly
characterized as erudite than as romantic.

The first, in C sharp minor, is an enormous cantabile for the
left hand, in dialogue with a less dominating cantabile on similar
thematic material for the right. Here there is no conflict between
technique and art: the technical purpose of the Étude is amply
fulfilled by the mere fact of its being the longest and most
elaborate cantabile ever written for the left hand; while as a work
of art it might perfectly well pass for one of Chopin's Nocturnes,
of which it would be among the largest and most beautiful.

As it is not only perfectly easy to follow but also fairly well
known and popular, quotations might seem unnecessary; but it
may not be amiss to illustrate one or two points in Chopin's art
which mere familiarity does not necessarily bring home to us,
though they are points which should deepen our admiration and
enjoyment.

The C sharp minor Étude, though a continuous stream of
melody, contains at least two distinct themes; the first—

Ex.1

being freely imitated by the right hand. The second theme in
the relative major which arises so beautifully from the prolonged
reluctance of the first—

Ex.2

stands alone, except for a solemn assent in the treble at the
cadence:

Ex.2a

From this point the movement digresses, passing with increasing passion through remote keys and culminating in a
stormy and majestic cadence in the extreme distance of E flat
major. After this crisis a wonderful quiet interlude, in which the
right hand has a pleading, aspiring cantabile, while the left
softly repeats again and again the phrase—

Ex.3

leads gradually to F natural major (as flat supertonic of E) and
thence with a broken preparatory allusion—

Ex.4

resumes Ex. 2 in E major, with immense breadth of effect, since
the whole of the previous far-reaching middle section now
appears closely welded to the great opening strain. With the last
bar of Ex. 2 we return to C sharp minor and the first theme,
which is now recapitulated with intensified touches. It leads once
more to Ex. 2, but this time in C sharp minor (thus giving somewhat the force of the 'second subject' of a sonata movement),
and with a pathetic reiteration of its second group—

Ex.5

passes into a short coda, which is the most truly classical touch
in a truly classical movement. The expected cadence is interrupted by that very chord with which Bach, Beethoven, and
Brahms so often defer the close of slow movements in a minor
key, a seventh on the tonic with a gleaming major third that the
dissonance (with its tendency towards the subdominant) gain-
says, like hope belied in the very moment of its expression:

Ex.6

Compare the last few bars of Bach's E flat minor Prelude
(*Wohltemperirte Clavier*, First Book, No. 8), the slow movement
of Beethoven's Pianoforte Sonata, op. 106, fourteen bars before
the end; the slow movement of Brahms's Quintet, op. 111, last
six bars; and other cases too numerous to mention. The present

example is all the finer for its coming as the only break in the extremely regular four-bar rhythm of the whole Étude (except for the unbarred introduction with which this regularity again forms an artistic contrast). Herein perhaps lies the only feature of the work (except matters of external style and, perhaps, emotional content) that is specifically romantic rather than classical. The only classical composer whose bar-rhythms are (except in fugues) as rigid as those of the romanticists is their great model Bach, whose works both Chopin and Schumann 'treated as their daily bread'. Haydn, Mozart, and Beethoven, except when writing variations or other kinds of work where great uniformity was desirable, made their phrases of every conceivable different length; and much of the eternal vigour and life of their works (and of Brahms's also) lies in the endless variety and interchange of quite ordinary rhythms as of other unobtrusive resources.

With the rise of lyric music, more rigid bar-rhythm (such as would soon become stiff if worked on a larger scale) became desirable as a framework for the freely-used small cross-rhythms and arabesques within the bars, and the constant use of tempo rubato; and hence the vast majority of Chopin's compositions are in almost unbroken four- and eight-bar rhythms, except in certain larger organisms such as the F minor Ballade, where his artistic instinct leads him to articulate his phrases almost as freely as Mozart—who constantly finds his bars at odds with the ever-changing lengths of his phrases.

I am only too well aware that all this is in flat contradiction to Received Impressions; but that is only because at present Receivers of Impressions are so much less intimately acquainted with classical music than the Romanticists were.

To return to Chopin's Études: the two next on our group may speak for themselves after the long analysis I have given of the C sharp minor. In the D flat Étude, the technical problem is the combination of staccato and legato in the same hand and *with the same rhythm*, a problem that involves no artistic difficulties, though, as far as I am aware, Chopin is the only important writer who has systematized it in its extreme form—most pianoforte educators having contented themselves with the simpler problem of rapid staccatos combined with a slow legato.

As this D flat Étude is the gayest and slightest of the group of three to which it belongs, let me take the opportunity of protesting against the common idea that that group contains only the weakest of Chopin's Études. I cannot but think that even this D flat one is altogether on a higher plane than several of the lighter ornaments in the two great sets, far richer and more delicate, for example, than those in F major and D flat, op. 25, nos. 3 and 8, or even than the G sharp minor and the two deservedly popular ones in G flat.

Our next Étude, in F minor, is a very beautiful and touching lyric, profoundly melancholy like the C sharp minor, and further resembling that in the holding in reserve for the last line a very beautiful piece of dark and warm harmonic colouring. Also, as in the C sharp minor (though on a much smaller scale), its continuous flow may be analysed into two themes—or rather two incidents, only just sufficiently differentiated to make the allusion, in the last line, to the second one, a thing to be felt rather than recognized.

It is interesting to note the influence of this impressive little lyric on Schumann in the third of his beautiful and most unaccountably neglected Four Fugues, op. 72:

Ex.7

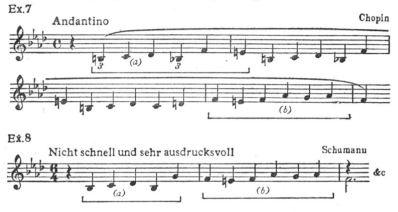

Who can hope to cure an indolent and inattentive aesthete of his folly if he cannot find a stimulus even in the spectacle of the most fantastic dreamer of the Romantic school basing his art on Bach, and the greatest and most sympathetic of Romantic pioneers borrowing that dreamer's themes to write fugues with?

As an Étude the little F minor presents no conflict of interests; being, like its lighter twin brother, op. 25, no. 2, simply a study in cross-rhythms, which fact leaves it as free as our C sharp minor movement to take its place high among the Nocturnes or Preludes.

Our last Étude, the great C minor, op. 25, no. 12, on the other hand, presents us with the most formidable possible type of the artistic problems that beset the Étude-writer. It treats of a peculiar form of arpeggio, both hands moving parallel and in unbroken semiquavers—perpetual motion. Now, in writing any kind of artistic *perpetuum mobile* on a large scale, even with free and thematic material such as that of Weber's Moto Perpetuo in the C major Sonata, the main difficulty arises from the absolute

M

uniformity of rhythm (at all events within the bar) which the mere fact of perpetual motion implies. And this difficulty is not lessened when the rapid notes are not themes but mere arpeggio forms that convey nothing by themselves but depend on their grouping for their meaning. Unless we can count a solitary and rather interesting prelude in F minor by Beethoven, Bach was the only great composer before Chopin who made really rich music on a single pattern-figure of uniformly flowing rhythm. Bach's simplest arpeggio-preludes in the *Wohltemperirtes Clavier* (e.g., the first and second) are among the best known of any, and it is interesting to see how far Chopin has followed them, and to ask ourselves why he has differed from them.

The only important difference (beyond self-evident matters of style and range) that I can discover is that Bach carefully avoids accidental resemblances to a square-cut tune in the general outline of his arpeggio groups, just as a skilled prose writer avoids accidental approaches to the rhythm of verse; whereas Chopin purposely makes his arpeggios form a tune, though one of severe simplicity and inexorable dignity. Both artists have solved their problem in the most perfect way their material would permit. For Bach, where rhythm was at a minimum, it was right that melody should also be at a minimum, and the instrumental effect of his arpeggios, though perfectly and delightfully characteristic of his clavichord, was not startling or exciting. With Chopin, on the other hand, the instrumental effect is of an exceptional and extremely luxurious kind; and for him it would be sheer vulgarity to display it without the substance of some clear melodic organization, and, if possible (since this rich instrumental effect needs a heightening of all other more intellectual resources that the case admits), some large rhythmic organization as well.

Chopin accordingly throws his emotional expression into the harmony rather than the melody (how different from the spirit of a certain popular sentimental melody written on the serene harmonies of Bach's first Prelude!), and with one of those extraordinary strokes of genius that analysis can partly discover but can never help to produce, makes his first grand piece of harmonic expression the very means of securing the desired variety of rhythm.

Here is Chopin's widespread arpeggio formula—

Ex.9

and here is the melodic outline which he makes it produce in the
first eight bars—

Ex.10

where a fresh rhythmic element already appears. Seven bars
later, Chopin bursts into the major, and at the thrill of the major
chord the arpeggios leap up an octave farther than before. This
naturally delays the descent, so that they touch ground a crotchet
late, and from the resulting new rhythm springs a second theme,
of which this is the outline:

Ex.11

How this is at once repeated with broad and deep effect in the
lower key of A flat; how the following surging passage leads with
ruthless leisureliness back to C; how the opening is recapitulated
and the C major outburst is delayed and expanded and made to
bring the work to a worthy end; and how the whole thing, with
all its immense harmonic power and brilliance, does not contain
a single chromatic chord, or a single chord that is not common
in Handel, or even perhaps Corelli, or a single change of tonic,
except that to the very closely related key A flat, as mentioned
above: these, and a small volume-full of similar points, must be
left to speak for themselves. We have taken a glance at the
greatest Étude of the greatest of Étude-writers, and we know that
he is a man as well as a dreamer.

15. IMPROMPTU IN F SHARP MAJOR, OP. 36, FOR PIANOFORTE

(1900)

THE 'Romantic' composers are generally most classical when
they are most free in form. If the word 'classical' has any meaning that is independent of custom and convention, it must mean
a specific form of 'maturity'; the condition of things in which the
style is the straightforward result of the matter, and the matter
is self-consistent and more or less such as would seem to the
plain man suitable for artistic treatment. 'Romantic' and other
reactions generally mean the search for new material in quarters
which artists have either never explored or have long neglected;
and hence it is probable that if any 'romantic' composition

radically differs from a classic, the difference will be in the use of material that the classical composer would not merely ignore but actually regard as unsuitable for artistic treatment.

Now this is seldom if ever true of Schumann and Chopin. Their material would certainly seem largely unfamiliar to an older classical composer, but there is no question of its capacity for artistic treatment; and if the material is new it must follow as the night the day that the treatment must be new also. Further, if the material is new, that can only be because it is not so readily conceived as that which occurs to the classical composer. It demands more familiarity with the more artificial aspects of human life; the modern novelist, for example, is given to demanding of the reader that he shall not expect the hero to express essentially heroic sentiments in language artistically fitted to their dignity when his origin and dialect are supposed to be humble. He must show his heroism through his own dialect, be it cockney or cultured slang, and we are apt to think that this simplifies the artistic novelist's aesthetic problems, whereas it is really an exceptionally difficult addition to their complexity. To a great artist the 'classical' method—that in which the diction is exactly what one might expect of the sentiment—is far more simple; the other method, that which makes the diction square with what we happen to know of human society, may be easier to read but needs justifying by an infinity of new artistic devices, most of which are not so much as intended to enter the reader's mind.

Chopin's Mazurkas, for example, are fairly popular, though their popularity is as nothing compared to their depth and flawlessness: but they are very dangerous things to misunderstand, with their extraordinary poise between colloquiality and erudition, irony and cordiality. What makes such 'romantic' works at once most purely artistic (or 'classical'), and most misleading to a hasty or flippant critic, is that the artist, working in the true classical spirit, compensates for these inherent difficulties and complexities in his material by an extreme clearness and simplicity of form: so that from the ordinary academic point of view the works seem childish and slight, and are often treated as such, to what has been well called the lamentable 'debasement of the moral currency'.

It is sometimes a positive relaxation to turn from such smaller and popular, but aesthetically complex works, to some hardly less popular, equally modern, but larger work like Chopin's F sharp major Impromptu. When Chopin writes in larger than lyric forms, he either produces something essentially non-classical with the old classical tonality and outline, as in his Concertos and Variations, or else something essentially classical in more or less free forms, as in the present impromptu, the Fantasia, op. 45, the Ballades, and the Études: except in the rare cases where a classical form will lend itself to a 'romantic' idea, as in the first two Scherzos. But he is usually most classical in free forms, because these have shaped themselves from the new material, just as the old classical forms shaped themselves from their own. And, lastly, we most readily feel this classical quality as such where Chopin is most essentially a dreamer of dreams; for there he has no motive for those colloquialities and ironies that often tend to make us so vividly misunderstand modern art. He takes us back into a world where everything is literal just because everything is fabulous. There is neither humour nor lack of humour, and brilliance is a sign of pure enjoyment, not a mask for bitterness of soul.

If we were given an abstract statement of the form, proportions, rhythms, keys, and contrasts of the F sharp major Impromptu, the chances are that we should suppose that we had been given an analysis of some newly-discovered movement by Beethoven in his 'third period', or Brahms. The crowd of pregnant themes, of every degree of length, from the opening cantabile:

Ex.1

with its preliminary and simultaneous counterpoint in the bass, to the single cadence-figure—

Ex.2

the 'interrupted close' into D major, with the central episode, so sharply and grandly contrasted with the rest—

Ex.3

—all these are features that, regarded apart from the intensely Chopinesque language of the whole, might easily be mistaken for the features of a Beethoven movement, especially the last-mentioned interrupted close, which indeed actually occurs in precisely the same form at something like half the breaks into fresh scenes in Beethoven's *Fidelio*.

It is with the finest judgement that Chopin, after this D major episode, returns to the first theme—not in the tonic, F sharp, but a semitone lower, in the extremely distant key of F natural. Chopin has already suggested, but is still holding in reserve, a characteristically modern brilliance of instrumental effect, and this instrumental brilliance must be balanced by a corresponding development of more intellectual harmonic resources, which in their turn have already been balanced by the very startling and dramatic contrast between the main themes and the D major episode.

After the first theme, its left-hand counterpoint ingeniously arpeggiated in triplets, has thus entered in its distant key, Chopin makes it shift easily round to the original tonic, F sharp, and there begins it again, the triplet variation now pervading the right hand as well as the left. In the course of this there appears what for a moment sounds like one of his characteristic free-rhythmed arabesques on the surface of the melody; but before we have time to realize what is happening it develops into a long running passage of entirely new material, which serves the manifold purposes of a new poetic surprise, a streak of brilliant tone-colour, a restoring of tonal balance by throwing all the weight of its unexpected entry on to the main chords of the tonic, and a means of isolating and delaying (and so emphasizing) the group of final cadence-themes. After this extraordinary cadenza (with its crowded harmonies that change almost with every quaver) has floated away, the slower and simpler cadence-themes enter with great breadth and quietness of effect —to be cut short by two vigorous final chords.

The custom of playing these two chords pianissimo originates from great authorities; but one may perhaps be pardoned for saying that it is very far from an improvement on Chopin's text. Soft chords here make a purely conventional end, and are essentially prosaic. Chopin's fortissimo awakening shows that, according to his way of thinking, a beautiful dream should not make one discontented with daylight.

BRAHMS

16. VARIATIONS AND FUGUE ON A THEME BY HANDEL, OP. 24, FOR PIANOFORTE

(1922)

THIS work ranks with the half-dozen greatest sets of variations ever written. As with every art-form Brahms treated, it represents a rediscovery of the fundamental principles of the form. Such rediscoveries are not to be achieved by academic mastery and tradition. It is the inevitable tendency of school tradition to descend to the level of average talent and average needs. The forms taught in the text-books are the forms which the majority of students can be trained to produce fairly well. It is a great mistake to call such forms classical; no work of art ever survived to become a classic unless it was from the outset an individual. The first maxim which must be realized by any one who wishes to understand the principles of works of art that have permanent value is that in art any average is probably false; that is to say, it is almost a mathematical impossibility that an individual work of art should in every single particular happen to coincide with any scheme deducible as an average from the generality of works of its type.

The habit of speaking of art-forms in general terms blinds us to the rarity of the specimens. Probably there is a greater number of immortal classical works in sonata form than in any other art-form. Perhaps there may be as many as five hundred classical sonatas, ranging from pianoforte solos to symphonies and concertos, including serenades, 'classical' meaning not compositions of a certain period, but compositions that can be enjoyed for their own sake at a concert without need for apologetic explanations as to their historic interest. This, however, is a very large estimate; but obviously any animal or flower of which the specimens were only to be counted by the five hundred would be considered a rarity: and when we come to the more special art-forms, such as the variation form, the rarity becomes extreme. Nobody knows, or wants to know, of any set of variations between Beethoven and Brahms, except seven specimens by Schumann, three by Mendelssohn, and two and a fragment by Chopin. Not even the whole of this handful is indispensable to musical salvation, and none of it is in the direct line of musical evolution. Beethoven had so astonished his own and the succeeding generation by the boldness of his ideas in variations as in other forms, that both Schumann and Mendelssohn failed to realize the fact

167

that Beethoven's variation form is about as accurate and concentrated as the closest of Bach's fugues. Schumann would write as a variation something of which he himself knew only that it sounded as unlike the theme as some of Beethoven's variations; and he actually did not know that the relation between Beethoven's freest variations and his theme is of the same order of microscopical accuracy and profundity as the relation of a bat's wing to a human hand. In other words Schumann goes and writes a beautiful independent episode and calls it a variation, whereas Beethoven writes real variations of the most accurate kind and makes them sound as fresh as independent episodes. Mendelssohn, in his few sets of variations, which were all poured out on one occasion with great zest (they are all mentioned in a single letter as written one after the other, including the set known as the *Variations Sérieuses*), was not in the least influenced by Beethoven's variations, though he knew them and delighted in them. His scheme is outwardly an enlargement of Mozart's idea of a set of variations. Inwardly, however, it is nothing of the kind. If Mozart generally sticks closely to the melodic outline of the theme, he includes therein all its deeper framework; this would be still more obviously the case if he did what Beethoven did on one impressive occasion (the Allegretto of the Seventh Symphony)—simply repeated his theme unvaried three times in a crescendo. But Mendelssohn produces ornamentation of the melody and lets the framework go to pieces. Again and again he gives you a version of the melody which goes on a different plan for no particular reason: the result being very little more than what would become of a Mozart set of variations if a person with immense talent tried to reproduce it by ear and forgot the theme while he was doing so. It is far better to follow Schumann, and produce under the name of variations something which is a delightful and inventive alternation between variations, discursive paragraphs on the melody, and independent episodes. This is a form which can stand on its merits; and the question of whether it has been given its right name is a mere question of philology.

The same may be said of the most recent developments of variation form. By all means let us have new forms, and let us not be shocked if the old name given to them is associated in the mind of scholars with something more highly (or at all events differently) organized. It is perhaps a slightly more interesting question whether these new forms are evolved from the classical main stem or not; but there again this does not concern their individual merit. There is, however, something to be said against a type of variation which really shows no reason for its line of variety beyond the apparent fact that the composer—

... cannot sing the old songs now!
It is not that he deems them low;
'Tis that he can't remember how
    They go.

One of the most interesting chapters in musical history is that
filled by the correspondence between the young Joachim and the
young Brahms, in which they sent each other compositions, and
recovered by discussion and practice the facts of the great classical art forms. The Variations on a Theme by Handel culminate
that chapter, and form one of the greatest monuments of clearness
and variety and that true freedom which consists in perfect fit-
ness and faithfulness to the matter in hand. All that is necessary
for the tracing of every fibre in the whole of this gigantic work
is to give a clear account of Handel's theme. I write it out with
its essential outlines in bolder notes than the ornamental version
in which Handel states it. All the miracles that happen in the
variations are traceable to the phenomena of this theme. Of
course, no such miracles are possible unless the theme has simple
and strong features and forms on which the variations can be
built. Let us, then, describe the theme as definitely as one can
describe such shapes in words.

Ex.1

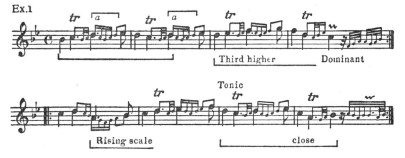

There is a simple two-bar phrase up and down the first four
notes of the scale, and ending with the mediant on the tonic
chord. This is answered by another two-bar phrase starting in
the same way on the third (or, melodically speaking, a third
higher) and brought to a half-close on the dominant. That
finishes the first part of the tune, which is repeated. The second
part of the tune, starting on the dominant with the same type of
rhythm, avoids coming to any sort of cadence in the second bar,
and rises in a longer scale to its top note, from which it drops to
a final phrase which is a kind of combination of the first and
second phrase, ending on the tonic. Thus the main features of
the theme are, in the first part the fact that the second phrase is
mostly a third higher than the first, and ends on the dominant

instead of the tonic; and, in the second part, the six notes of rising scale leading to the last two bars which close in the tonic.

The first variation humorously exaggerates and modernizes Handel's eighteenth-century ornamentation. It follows the melodic outline very closely in a lively staccato. The second variation is also melodic, and glides gracefully in smooth triplets with chromatic inner parts. The third variation treats the melody quietly and tenderly in sighing appoggiaturas in dialogue between the right hand and the left. Variation 4, while sticking close to the melody, thunders along in semiquaver chords, with strong accents off the beat. The rising scale in the second part is harmonized in a key related to the tonic minor, a foreshadowing of greater harmonic freedom hereafter. Now comes a quiet variation in the minor; and here in the second strain we begin to notice the signs of a broader conception of the possibilities of the theme, for the second strain is not only a third higher melodically but starts in a key a third higher, D flat, coming round quite easily to its half-close on the dominant; and the second part very happily begins on the chord of F minor instead of the ordinary major chord on F as dominant. The next variation is, as happens frequently in great sets of variations on so short a theme, a sequel to this—a variation of a variation. It takes the special melodic figures of its predecessor and moves darkly and mysteriously in close canon between the right hand and the left. Here again the second phrase is not only a third higher, but in the key of D flat. In the second part the left hand leads and the right hand answers in contrary motion.

In the next pair of variations, we return to the major, with a lively anapaest rhythm. Here again, in Variation 7, the key of D minor appears as a translation of the fact that the second phrase is a third higher than the first. In the eighth variation the anapaest rhythm is kept up in perpetual drumming on the tonic and the dominant throughout. Variation 9 works out the use of the key a third higher in the first part, in sublime style as one of the harmonic miracles in the work, answering the first phrase in B flat by its plain repetition in the bright key of D. The second part simplifies matters by merely answering two bars of dominant by two bars of tonic; but in repeating this another miracle takes place, completing that of the first part, for instead of the dominant we have a chord or key a semitone higher (G flat). Variation 10 humorously scatters the outline of the melody down four octaves of the pianoforte, disappearing into the minor mode as it touches bottom. Variation 11 blossoms out in a delightful kind of Handelian urbanity, combined with full realization of modern variation-writing, inasmuch as the second phrase not only takes the key of D minor as the equivalent of going a third higher, but actually closes on its dominant chord (A major). Variation 12 gives most of the outline of the melody to the left hand, while nightingales sing above.

Variation 13 is in the minor. It suggests a kind of Hungarian funeral march, again treating the key of D flat as the equivalent to going a third higher.

Variations 14, 15, 16, 17, and 18 arise one out of the other in a wonderful decrescendo of tone and crescendo of romantic beauty. Variation 14 is in a mood of blustering energy and gives great prominence to the turn on the third beat of the melody (Ex. 1, Fig. (a)). This turn forms the main idea of the next variation, in the second part of which we have the only case where the framework has been stretched. (The rising scale happens to be proceeding chromatically instead of diatonically, and this causes a bar's delay.) Variation 16 is a mysterious pianissimo and staccato parody of its predecessor, in dialogue between the right hand and the left. From its initial two notes Variation 17, in a slightly quicker tempo, derives an incessant dropping staccato figure while the outline of the melody is heard in elfland horns in the inner parts. This outlined melody takes a firmer consistency in the next variation where it is surrounded above and below with delicate arpeggios bringing this group of five variations to its romantic end.

Variation 19 saunters along its placid way in 12/8 time (a quick Siciliana rhythm) in an inner part. Variation 20 harmonizes the melody in chromatic chords which reach a wonderful depth of remoteness; it is the most solemn passage in the whole work. Variation 21 surprises us with a change of key to G minor. The melodic outline remains untransposed, and can be detected as grace notes inside the triplet figure of the right hand. In its gentle plaintiveness it is a very refreshing and beautiful reaction from its solemn predecessor. Variation 22 is a charming grotesque on a drone bass, high in pitch and full of humour. Variations 23 and 24 are a menacing crescendo in excited 12/8 rhythm, swarming up energetically out of darkness. Variation 25 is a triumphant climax in the most brilliant full harmony. And now we break away naturally into freedom from the cycle of the theme in which we have accomplished these twenty-five revolutions. There is no feeling of break, for the mighty fugue which now begins is on a subject which consists of the first two bars of the theme:

Ex.2

It is admirably clear and easy to follow, especially in view of the wonderful breadth of the slow diminuendos to an intense pianissimo as the work reaches its climax. It may be as well to quote two of the main incidents in its growth; first the inversion of the theme and secondly its augmentation:

Ex.3

At the great final climax the countersubject, which I indicated in quoting the theme, develops into very prominent running sequences in the right hand which I quote in their last phase, where they are inverted while the main theme proceeds in dialogue both inverted and direct:

Ex.5

One of the most wonderful features of the whole work and of this climax in particular is the perfect accuracy with which everything is conveyed in terms of a pianoforte style which, though by no means easy, is entirely free from artificiality or makeshift. Intrinsic difficulty is another matter; but for pure economy of means Brahms's Variations on a Theme by Handel are as perfect a specimen of the treatment of their instrument as is to be found in art.

17. VARIATIONS ON A THEME BY PAGANINI, OP. 35, FOR PIANOFORTE

(1900)

THESE variations are, so far as I know, unique in being divided into two sets which, while intimately connected and forming a single process of development, are nevertheless two complete and

independent works. On any given occasion it is best to play one
of these two sets singly; but as they illustrate each other, I here
analyse both.

The theme comes from one of Paganini's best displays of
violin virtuosity, where it is also used for variations, a purpose
for which it is admirably suited. Some of Paganini's own variations on it are distinctly good; and indeed there are faint resemblances between some of his violin figures and the gorgeous
rhythmic and instrumental effects and tone-colours in which
these of Brahms are so rich. The melodic interest of the theme
is slight, but it is not on melodic resemblance that the present
type of variation depends. These are harmonic and rhythmic
variations, such as Bach gave us in his immense set of thirty (the
'Goldberg' Variations) or Beethoven in his thirty-three on a
waltz of Diabelli. The qualities essential to a theme for such a
set are a strong, clear, and conclusive harmonic basis, with a bar-
rhythm to match. Great melodic interest is, no doubt, welcome,
but not so necessary as in the type of variation-movement that
sometimes occurs in sonatas—where the whole style is necessarily far more dependent on thematic identity in the melodic
sense. But in a large self-contained set of variations, it is often
a powerful means of effect that some of the variations should be
more melodious than the theme; and in any case the composer's
problem is not—as in a sonata-movement set—to aim at frequent
reminders of the outline of a single beautiful melody, but rather
to produce a developing series of different ideas on a single harmonic and rhythmic plan.

Here is the first part of Paganini's theme (right hand only) as
Brahms states it:

Ex.1.

The grace-notes, which give the theme most of its light and
capricious character, are added by Brahms.

The second part of the theme is on the same figure. To save
trouble I give its harmonic basis only:

Ex.1a

It is important to notice the rhythmic structure of this second part, as it is the one infallible thread in the most free and rich of the variations. As shown here by the figures, first there are two steps of descending sequence, each step being two bars long: then two further descending steps, each one bar long: lastly, a cadence in which two harmonies are crowded into the penultimate bar.

Looking back on the whole theme we may expect to find that the first part will be treated with some freedom, since it consists of a mere alternation of tonic and dominant. That alternation is so far the simplest fact in all tonality that the ear will accept almost any other alternation of important functional chords as a paraphrase of it; and hence we shall find, as we proceed, a large variety of other forms of alternation and other radical chords used to replace this extremely simple basis of the theme. In the second part there is more variety, but the sequential structure is so strong and clear that it will be recognized even where all the harmonies are altered, and we may actually find a variation in which hardly any of the original harmonies and absolutely nothing of the original melody can be traced, while yet the structure remains so unmistakably and characteristically the same that there is no difficulty in tracing the connexion with the theme. Here we have one of the great differences between truly artistic variations and those of the intelligent composer who searches for freedom and finds it not. He fails because he thinks of the details of melody, harmony, and rhythm, but forgets that his theme also has a broad and easily recognized structure that is independent of these details—unless indeed the theme is his own invention, in which case it very possibly has no such structure. The result is that such a composer, in his most unrestrained variations, does not attain such contrast and remoteness from the outward surface of his theme as does the great composer; nor are the simplest of the merely clever composer's variations such vivid embodiments of the structure of his theme as are the most remote of the great composer's.

The other main point in which Brahms shows himself one of the truly great composers is the coherence of his whole sets as schemes of contrast and climax—a matter in which the ordinary (or even extraordinary) clever variations of modern times are apt to be amazingly deficient. Brahms's dramatic skill I leave to illustrate itself in the course of following the first set by itself as a complete work, to begin with.

After the playful, mocking tone of the theme, Brahms plunges into variations laid out on a large scale. He wishes to make it clear that this very slight theme is to be the foundation of a serious work, and accordingly he begins with a pair of variations —the first in sixths for the right hand—

Ex 2

and the second consisting of the same material for the left hand. Though severely simple, and absolutely faithful to the harmonies of the theme, these variations (especially the second) have minute touches of detail that prevent them from becoming monotonous. But no modern composer but a very great one would have dared to write two such simple variations together. Now that we see it done, it is clear to us that this beginning with a pair of variations on one severely simple idea is the broadest and most dignified opening that could have been devised. With the third variation comes our first change of rhythm— to 6/8 time:

Ex.3

Here we see chromatically descending steps in harmonic skeleton—

Ex.3a

inserted between the original plain tonic (*T*) and dominant (*D*). The repeats are given with fresh touches.

The fourth variation, though again in a new time—12/16— pairs with the third in its fan-like figure-work and its insertion of descending steps between tonic and dominant in the first part:

Ex.4

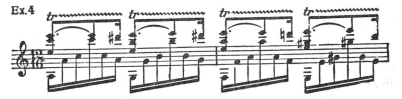

In the repeats the right and left hands change parts.

This completes Brahms's exordium. He has by this time established one of the important elements in the tone and range of these variations, viz., an extreme brilliance of instrumental colour. This is what we might have expected from the theme; which, with its mocking character, could hardly be given a large and broad development without the aid of this appeal to the senses. The superb reserve and dignity with which Brahms embodies his first instrumental effects in a great block of four variations of extreme simplicity and impassive character, thoroughly prevents any possibility of the brilliance sinking into mere virtuosity or even suggesting it to an attentive and impartial listener.

It is now time for this impassive manner to give way to more direct appeals to the feelings. The fifth variation has an expressive, sweeping melody for the right hand—

Ex.5a

with a syncopated rising chromatic scale in contrary (6/8) rhythm for the left:

Ex.5b

That is the gist of it, but the left hand part is broken and scattered through different octaves, rapidly crossing and recrossing over the right, thus:

Ex 5c

The effect is very novel and kaleidoscopic, and combines with the plaintive part of the right hand to make this variation an appropriate sequel as well as an effective contrast to the combination of severity and brilliance which characterized the preceding four. It will be seen that the first part alternates the *keys* of E and A minor in pairs of bars, instead of the *chords* of tonic and dominant in single bars. The second part is strict.

The sixth variation is far more plaintive, and shows a melodic resemblance to the theme in the left hand. Note the strange and wayward free augmentation in the right hand:

Ex.6

The harmonies are strictly those of the theme.
In the seventh variation—

Ex.7

Left hand in contrary motion

the pent-up passions break forth. Still, the harmonies are quite
strict, as they also are in the eighth variation, in spite of the
powerful and fierce effect of the bold auxiliary notes (*) resolved
in a lower octave (†):

Ex.8

The ninth variation plunges into a dramatic and weird mood
of terror and power. It is extremely free in harmony. In the
first part a chord of F is substituted for the chord of A in the
first and third bars, and a chord of C for E in the fourth bar. In
the second part the descending sequences pass through an entirely new and remote set of keys, beginning with G minor and
F minor; but the structure—two bars, two bars, one bar, one
bar, and two bars of cadence with crowded harmony—remains
as clear as in the theme, while the effect of the new harmony is
immensely rich and deep. Here is the beginning of the variation:

Ex.9

As this is exactly half the pace of the preceding group, the
throbbing bass carries on the 6/8 rhythm of the preceding group
of variations. In the second part the right hand has the throbbing, while the left hand has descending semiquavers that correspond to the ascending ones in the quotation.

The storm dies away, and the next variation is a subdued and
sad brooding, lightly scored and not without spring in its rhythm,

N

but melancholy and pathetic. The harmonies are strict—two
bars corresponding to one of the theme:

Ex.10

The last chord is major, and is marked with a pause. The
eleventh variation, slow and in the major mode, comes as an absolute contrast and relief, completely unmasking the deep human
feeling that underlies all the brilliance, wit, and grimness of these
sets of variations:

Ex 11

The harmonies are strict, except for translation into the new
relationship of A major, from which some rich effects result.

Ethereal and romantic as this is, the twelfth variation is yet
more so:

Ex.12

In the first part tonic and dominant are alternated in a different
way from that of the theme. In the second part the harmonies
are as strict as the change of mode admits. One of the most
remarkable things about this wonderfully original and beautiful
variation is that it is in strict canon in the octave at a quaver's
distance throughout, the right-hand part being disguised only by
broken octaves and triplet motion. If the reader will look at the
quotation, omitting the first note of each triplet, this will become
self-evident. The disguise is a great stroke of genius, at once
preventing the canon from sounding academic and producing a
cross-rhythm and a beautiful instrumental effect.

From this Brahms awakes as from a lovely dream, and the
thirteenth variation is sardonic laughter of the most audacious

kind. It will speak for itself, without need of quotation. Its
shrill octaves and its tearing octave glissandos mark it as the
humorous forerunner of some stormy, blustering finale; and
indeed the last variation (the last with a number, for the coda
contains more, as is very frequent in harmonic sets) bursts out
like a hurricane—

(*y*) may or may not refer to the melody of the theme.
Like the preceding variation this is faithful to the harmonic
framework of the theme; but Brahms secures a most startling
effect by displacing the repeat of the first part on to the dominant
of C sharp minor:

The strictly harmonized second part follows this quite naturally, but the plunge into distance and back again is of grand
effect. The variation passes into a coda with increasing bustle
and energy, till it comes to a pause, and then begins to work out
the figure here marked (*x*), as follows—

and in canon, thus:

This passage has a slight suggestion of being the beginning of
a new variation on the harmonic transformation exemplified in
Variation 4, but it does not go far enough to establish itself. The
figure (*x*) becomes rapidly filed down, thus—

to a trill between the two hands, and on this arises a final variation—

strict in harmony, which in an expanded coda rushes headlong
to a passionate and spirited close.

The second set may be said, in a sense, to begin where the
first left off, though it is also a perfectly complete and independent
work. But it begins with a harmonic freedom much like that
which was so startling in the fourteenth variation of the first set;
and it plunges at once into a most impassioned storm, which is
the more effective from the fact that the theme is stated very
quietly and delicately. Brahms thus makes his second set intelligible from two points of view—as a further development from
the first set, and as an independent work, opening on the opposite system to that of the first set. Whereas the first set opens
broadly with a large block of simple and severe variations to pave
the way for the more elaborate and impassioned, the second set
opens dramatically with some of its most free and impassioned,
designed to tone down, as the passion exhausts itself, into simpler
variations that embody the exact harmonies of the theme.

Here is the opening of the first variation, in slower bars than
those of the theme:

These first two bars embody the tonic and dominant in sufficiently clear alternation, but the fourth bar substitutes the distant dominant of C sharp minor, with gorgeous effect. The whole variation is in double counterpoint; that is to say, the themes of the right and left hand, $\left\{\begin{array}{l}a\\b\end{array}\right.$ are repeated in reversed position, $\left\{\begin{array}{l}b\\a\end{array}\right.$

The second part emphasizes the characteristic structure of the theme, its descending sequences in steps of two bars, two bars, one bar, one bar, and a crowded cadence; but it carries the process further, and through extremely distant keys, thus:

> 2 bars, D minor; 2 bars, C minor; 1 bar, B flat minor; 1 bar, A flat minor; ½ bar, F sharp minor; ½ bar, E major as dominant; Cadence, A minor and major.

The second variation is comparatively simple, but grandly impassioned:

Ex.17

It substitutes two other chords for the dominants in the second and fourth bars, but the second part is strict in harmony.

The third variation laughs the passion down, with a certain tenderness in its brilliance:

Ex.18

In the first part subdominant harmonies are substituted in bars 2 and 3, and in the second part the descending and diminishing sequences are carried further into half-bars, as in the first variation, but without any remote tonality. The epigrammatic utterances of the bass, as indeed of the whole variation, should be carefully noted.

The fourth variation is an exquisite little waltz (3/8 time) in the major, so delightful and clear, and (like all the next seven variations) so strictly on the harmonies of the theme, that I leave it without quotation. The fifth variation resumes the minor mode; and, but for a most effective substitution of the chord of C for the dominant in the fourth bar, is strict as to harmony.

The sixth variation is a simple harmonic skeleton of the theme in triplet arpeggios with grace-notes before each triplet.

The seventh variation is absolutely strict and simple, but may be quoted in outline for its extraordinary contrary rhythm:

Ex.19

Like the first, this is in double counterpoint, the hands exchanging themes as it proceeds.

In the eighth variation Brahms gives a choice between a very simple form in staccato arpeggios ('quasi pizzicato' and somewhat resembling one of the variations in Paganini's own set) and a more thematic idea in the same rhythm. From the ordinary academic point of view the latter variation might seem preferable, but Brahms does not take the ordinary academic point of view. He gives the simpler variation in the large type, and the other as an alternative in smaller type below. This is the only case within my knowledge where a composer has had such wealth of ideas for variations that he is forced to use one of them as a mere alternative to another one; and it is doubly remarkable, coming in a work that is already divided into two independent sets, because the material is too voluminous to be worked out on a single thread.

Here is a good opportunity for reflecting on the artistic and dramatic truth of the second set up to the eighth variation. A less great composer, furnished with all the skill that training can give, would have strained every nerve to follow up the first two variations (supposing those had been given him as a starting point) with further developments of passion and power. But Brahms knows—and helps us to see ourselves—that such a sudden storm of passion, bursting in after a light and unpretending theme is, alike from the aesthetic and ethical points of view, bound to spend itself as suddenly as it began; and he therefore follows it up with half-plaintive laughter and 'the uncertain glory of an April day'. The extremely strict and simple harmonization of the block of variations from the second part of the fifth to the end of the eighth is an equally appropriate reaction from the startling freedom of the stormy opening, and for precisely the same reason Brahms prefers the simpler form of the eighth variation and allows whole variations to pass by without any definite melodic idea, like very short and unpretending arpeggio movements of the type of Bach's first Prelude in the *Wohltemperirtes Clavier*. In analysing variations we are too apt to take them as so many independent organisms of which the least elaborate is necessarily the least worthy of its position; and this very elementary mistake (how elementary it seems when we see the drastic way in which Brahms, in the present work, counteracts any such tendency!)—this mistake is at the root of the failure of half the clever variation-writing and criticism of the present day.

After the airy texture and simple material of this large block of variations, the pent-up passions break out again—suddenly and fiercely. The ninth variation is still strict in harmony, but makes a tremendous noise with its lumbering, weighty figure that sprawls over the whole keyboard. The tenth variation is also really strict in essential harmonic basis—the only radical freedom being the substitution of a diminished seventh for the tonic chords in the first part; but an amazingly rich and startling harmonic effect is produced by the long auxiliary notes before each essential chord, these auxiliary notes being by far the most emphatic in the bar, and combining with the rest of the real chord to give an illusion of other very distant harmonies, like C sharp minor, F sharp minor, &c. I quote the first two bars of the second part:

Ex.20

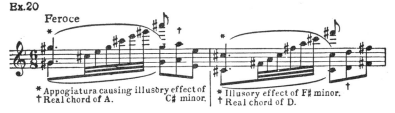

* Appogiatura causing illusory effect of
† Real chord of A.   C♯ minor.

* Illusory effect of F♯ minor.
† Real chord of D.

After this gorgeous outburst of rage, the fiercest we have yet witnessed, Brahms once more laughs it down in a light and rapid variation with a peculiar effect of mixed octaves, contrary motion, and a mood akin to that of one who mockingly sings the knell of a lost temper by a rapid recitation of 'Peter Piper picked a peck of pickled pepper'. Harmonies are clear and strict but for the splendidly rich chords of F sharp minor and E minor which are substituted for those of D and E in the second part.

But with all this mockery there is no lack of deep human sympathy in the world Brahms presents to us. As in the first set, here also the twelfth is a serene and lovely variation in the major; but, taking advantage of the wider range of harmonic freedom that characterizes the second set, Brahms here leaves the tonic of A, and puts this variation in F major—the first and only permanent change of key that has yet occurred.

Here are the first two bars—

Ex.21

and these embody the tonic and dominant as unmistakably as did the theme. That being so, Brahms calmly repeats the phrase a third lower, so that we still have a tonic and dominant, but a fresh one, that of D minor. The freedom is extremely bold and fresh in effect, but a perfectly clear and legitimate derivative from the structure of the theme. The second part is also translated somewhat freely, but the characteristic structure—descending sequence in steps of two bars, two bars, one bar, one bar, and a crowded cadence—is as unmistakable as ever.

This variation is too serious to be met with mockery, and the one that follows, with its return to the minor, is thoroughly pathetic:

Ex.22

Harmonies are comparatively strict, though the passing-notes are very poignant. One would hardly think that simple legato octaves for the right hand could be made to sound like a special effect; but in repeating the second part, Brahms secures this by introducing them as a contrast to the disguised octaves of the previous inner part. It is the great composer's privilege that he can make ordinary things tell.

In the next variation mockery returns; gentle and not unsympathetic, but still playful; with a laughing diminution of the drooping melody of the preceding variation:

Ex.23

Harmonies are strict now to the very end. Brahms is gathering up his threads for the conclusion.

This variation passes into three more—unnumbered by Brahms, and incomplete in so far as one passes into the next before forming a full close. Quotations are unnecessary, as rhythms and harmony are quite clear. The second of these extra variations is greatly expanded towards the close, and leads with a great crescendo to the final outburst, a fierce variation in 6/8 time which plunges, even more headlong than the coda of the first set, to the end of the most essentially brilliant set of variations that has ever taken its place among truly great works of art.

18. QUARTET IN G MINOR, OP. 25, FOR PIANOFORTE, VIOLIN, VIOLA,
AND VIOLONCELLO

(1901)

Allegro. G minor, C.
INTERMEZZO. *Allegro ma non troppo.* C minor, 9/8.
Andante con moto. E flat major, 3/4.
RONDO ALLA ZINGARESE. *Presto.* G minor, 2/4.

THE first movement opens with two broad melodies; one in the tonic—

Ex.1

and the other in the relative major:

Ex.2'

A short outburst on figure (*a*) (from No. 1) in B flat minor, leads angrily back to the tonic, where a fortissimo counterstatement of No. 1, combined with a new figure (*f*):

Ex.3

leads to the transition to the second subject; which, after an angry dialogue on figures (*f*) and (*a*), enters in D minor: beginning with the following melody for the violoncello:

Ex.4

After a counterstatement by the pianoforte, the cadence of this theme—

Ex.5

is worked up to a climax, culminating in a burst into D major, on figure (*f*) where a new derivative of (*g*) (see No. 4) appears, accompanied by (*f*):

Ex. 6

This leads to a new figure—

Ex.7

which closes in a great theme, whose present jubilant character will eventually prove a pathetic contrast to what it becomes at the end of the movement:

Ex.8

It will be seen that part of this theme is reminiscent of the ubiquitous figure (*f*)—by augmentation.

Suddenly there is a calm: a new figure, accompanied by the augmented version of (*f*), appears—

Ex.9

and, after an expanded counterstatement, closes in a long-drawn
cadence passage consisting of figures (*a*) and (*b*) from No. 1, in
the major and in dialogue between pianoforte and strings:

Ex.10

This, too, has an expanded counterstatement, which brings to a
close one of the most voluminous second subjects ever written.

The development opens, as so often where the exposition has
not been marked to be repeated, with the first theme (No. 1) in
the tonic as at the outset. No. 2 follows, however, in C minor,
and leads through a mysterious series of transitions (on figure
(*f*)) to A minor, where No. 1 is developed in the following four
ways: First, stormily, omitting the first note and combining
with (*f*):

Ex.11

Secondly, quietly, repeating each figure bar by bar, so as to turn
the first four bars of No. 1 into an eight-bar phrase, accompanied
by (*f*):

Ex.12

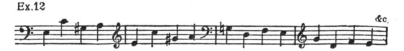

Thirdly, crescendo, as follows, (*f*) subsiding into a plain tremolo:
And, lastly, in three-part canon through many keys leading
stormily to the dominant of G, our original key:

Ex.13

Ex.14

The storm dies away, and we expect a return to the first subject in the minor as at the outset; but, with touching effect, No. 2
appears instead in the tonic major. It leads, however, back to
the stormy counterstatement No. 3, which in its turn leads to
the second subject—but not to No. 4. Instead, it plunges straight
into No. 6 in the new key of E flat. No. 7 follows passionately in
the tonic, G *minor*: and (a touch that makes this wonderfully rich
and dramatic movement really epoch-making) No. 8, formerly so
jubilant, is transformed into a quiet and most pathetic passage,
in the minor, thus—

Ex.15

and thus:

Ex.16

The sequels, Nos. 9 and 10, are also in the minor and of the
utmost poignancy, rising at the end to a passionate climax, after
which the movement dies down into darkness and silence.

The second movement (Intermezzo) corresponds to the classical scherzo and trio. Its first section announces the following
two themes—

Ex.17

and, in the dominant—

Ex.18

and a counterstatement, in which the pianoforte and strings change parts, leads to a largely proportioned new melody, beginning thus—

Ex.19

in F minor; in which key No. 17 reappears, leading by some very remarkable sequences to the dominant of C minor (the key of the movement) where we again have No. 19. This, expanded and continued in the major, leads to No. 18 in the tonic, which thus rounds off the form.

The trio then follows. It is somewhat faster, is in A flat major, and is strongly contrasted with the main section in its brightness and liveliness of tone: though the sense of mystery and romance is as strong as ever. Its principal theme is in disguised imitation between the pianoforte and violin.

Ex.20

In the second part of this trio the rhythm of the group marked (*a*) is taken to form a new theme, in the distant key of E natural (F flat) beginning thus:

Ex.21

(*9*)

This is brought back to A flat, and leads to No. 20 in D flat (the pianoforte part being at first displaced, so that it coincides with the violin instead of anticipating it), and a crescendo leads, through several keys, back to the dominant of C minor—with figure (*a*) from No. 20 in octaves returning reluctantly to the pathetic and mysterious main section (Nos. 17–18 and 19), which is repeated without alteration.

A short code in C major rounds off the movement with No. 20.

Like the Intermezzo, the slow movement is of the form A, B, A, but it has still more development. It begins (as was Brahms's usual practice at this period of his work—and as we have already seen in the first two movements) with a pair of contrasted themes.

The first is a broad melody beginning thus, in E flat:

Ex.22

The second begins on the dominant of G, thus—

Ex 23

and leads back to the first in E flat, which is repeated and brought to a close. This ends the first section of the movement. Then follows a large transition-section consisting of No. 22 in the bass, with a new melody above—

Ex.24.

alternating with No. 23. This leads to the dominant of C, where, with the accompaniment of a persistent rhythmic figure—

we have a long anticipatory passage founded on the following phrase in imitation—

Ex.25

and leading at last to the central episode in C major. This is very animated and stirring. The rhythmic figure becomes—

tossed from one instrument to the other, and serving as accompaniment to the following:

Ex.26

This is stated as a long rounded-off melody, entirely pianissimo, and dying away in the key in which it began. Suddenly it crashes out in A flat, and leads stormily to a fierce new theme in F minor:

Ex.27

This is thrown into three-part canon, and returns to C major, where No. 26 reappears fortissimo. It again leads to No. 27, and thence, after a solemn close, to the return of the first theme (No. 22) in C major. This soon shifts back to the tonic, E flat, where the whole first section is recapitulated with ornamental variation, and a short and solemn coda on Nos. 23 and 22 brings the movement to an end.

Beneath its simple, sectional exterior the Finale conceals a highly organized structure, containing in its final quasi-extempore cadenza the most elaborate piece of development in the quartet.

The opening pair of themes like the whole first section is in 3-bar rhythm.

Ex.28

The last notes of the final cadence—

Ex.30

give rise to a new theme:

Ex.31

which, after a remarkable digression to F sharp minor, returns to Nos. 28 and 29: which end in the final cadence quoted in No. 30.

Then follows the first episode, a running binary section in the relative major, B flat, and in 2-bar rhythm:

Ex.32   &c.

Both halves of this are repeated, and then the main section (Nos. 28–30) returns, varied towards the end by a decrescendo and an expansion of No. 30. This dies away, and the two cadence-notes (*a*) are suddenly turned into a new theme in the tonic major, constituting the first of a second episode:

Ex 33   (*a*)

This alternates with the following:

Ex.34

Then, when these two have been rounded off into a complete form, we have an episode within the episode. This is a large quasi-binary tune in E minor beginning thus:

Ex.35

This is followed, not by a return to No. 33, but by the surprising entry of No. 32 in the tonic major. This becomes combined with the first figure of No. 33, thus—

Ex.36   (a)

and leads back to Nos. 33 and 34 in full. The last two notes of this section happen to be the same as (a) of Nos. 30 and 31 with a trill. Accordingly, No. 32 reappears in the tonic minor with a trill and—this is an important point—*without alluding to the opening theme at all*, leads through No. 29 to an enormous cadenza in which the four instruments seem to extemporize on the central themes one by one, passing through many distant keys—

Ex.37

modulating to E minor.

Then the pianoforte appears alone with No. 32—

Ex 38

modulating to F sharp minor. The strings re-enter with No. 33 in angry canonic dialogue and rising sequence:

Ex.39

When they reach the dominant of G the pianoforte again appears with No. 32, the strings continuing with No. 33, thus producing the combination shown in No. 36. An exciting crescendo and quickening of time leads to the final return of the long-lost first theme, molto presto, and the end of the Quartet in high rage.

19. QUARTET IN A MAJOR, OP. 26, FOR PIANOFORTE, VIOLIN, VIOLA, AND VIOLONCELLO

(1901)

Allegro non troppo. A major, 3/4.
Poco Adagio. E major, C.
SCHERZO. *Poco Allegro.* A major, 3/4.
FINALE. *Allegro.* A major, ¢.

IN this, as in his nearly contemporaneous G minor Quartet, Brahms groups most of his themes in pairs; with a strong tendency towards working the two contrasted members of the pair into a complete binary organization in miniature. This device inevitably takes time, but, once grasped, it makes the elaborate and rich thematic material unusually easy to follow.

The opening of the first movement is typical. Its two themes—

Ex.1

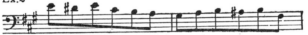

Ex.2

are at once repeated in a counterstatement, No. 2 being transposed to the tonic almost like a miniature second subject.

The counterstatement is expanded, and leads to a fortissimo passage on figure (*a*), which moves into the dominant, where we have a new theme in preparation for the second subject:

Ex.3

The second subject itself begins with another very complete and broadly designed organism containing the following figures:

Éx.4

194

Ex.5

Ex.6

It is grouped into 4-bar phrases of a regularity which should make it casy to follow, in spite of its exceptional richness. It is answered by a second part, which takes all the above three themes in the same order, beginning with No. 4 slightly altered, thus—

Ex.7

passing through G major, with No. 5, to E minor with No. 6, which becomes—

Ex.8

and leads through a most romantic diminuendo to an important new theme—

Ex.9

which, expanded and varied in semiquavers by the pianoforte, closes in the cadence subject.

This is derived from (c) of No. 5, and begins as follows:

Ex.10

It is taken up by the pianoforte, and its last bars—

Ex.11

are made to lead in the first instance back to the beginning of the movement for the repetition of the whole exposition, and in the second instance through a series of modulations into C major, thus merging insensibly into the development section.

This is founded mainly on the first subject, and is for a long time confined to the dark and remote key of C minor. (This device of making the development take place in some single and characteristically constructed key, instead of continually shifting, dates from the later works of Beethoven, and is very typical of Brahms. It is an inevitable artistic result of the large scale and manifold thematic material of such works as this quartet.)

The first theme is entirely changed in rhythm and character by the following variations—

Ex.12

Such lines of thematic treatment were first invented by Brahms. Their peculiarity is that, while they utterly change the whole tone and mood of the theme, they differ so slightly from their original note by note that no intermediate steps are possible; whereas before Brahms's work all notable thematic transformations were gradual, and by the time a radical difference was attained, there were many steps to remember in tracing the new version to its original.

Figure (*a*) is now worked up crescendo in both its new and its old forms, and gradually it leaves C minor, and, changed into the following phrase:

Ex.14

leads quickly to A minor, where the quiet theme No. 9 from the end of the second subject startles us by bursting in fortissimo, followed by the cadence-subject, No. 10. Over the close of this (No. 11) the strings and pianoforte have some discussion whether it should be major or minor. The pianoforte will have it minor, but the strings insist on major—rightly, since it is suddenly discovered that we have for some time been back in our original

tonic, as is shown by the calm appearance of the first subject at
the outset, an octave lower; thus beginning the recapitulation.

No. 2 appears in due course, alternating with No. 1 as before;
but in the counterstatement it modulates to C major, causing a
corresponding displacement of the sequel, which, however, leads
to the transition passage No. 3 in the tonic, followed in due
course by the whole second subject (Nos. 4–11), also in the tonic,
and unaltered except for a change in the assignment of themes
among the instruments at the outset. The counterstatement of
No. 10 modulates for a moment in a new direction, only to lead
to a quiet coda entirely in the tonic and founded on (*a*) of the
first theme; at first in canon, thus—

Ex.15

and afterwards as in No. 12, but in the major.

The slow movement is in E major, the dominant of the key of
the quartet. This relationship has the reputation of being unusual for middle movements: and in many cases one can understand that a middle movement in the dominant, where the first
movement had, as usual, its second subject in that key, might be
difficult to manage with due variety of tonal colouring. But
where the tendency to centralize the development in some single
distant key is as strong as in the present first movement, considerable definite tonal variety is already secured: and there is a certain familiar brilliance about the dominant as a key for middle
movements which makes it peculiarly attractive in effect.

In earlier classical days it was by no means so rare as is often
supposed. Haydn and Mozart use it more often than any other
key but the conventional subdominant; as a search through
Köchel's Catalogue and Haydn's Quartets will at once prove.

The present slow movement is a very large rondo. I quote the
themes, leaving the astonishing colouring to speak for itself.
The main theme is stated simultaneously in sustained outline and
quaver variation:

Ex.16

The quaver outline dies away into—

Ex.17

(a)

which modulates impressively through G minor and F minor, leading back to the rondo theme varied thus:

Ex.18

As before, the theme dies away into figure (a) of No. 17. This time, however, there are no arpeggios; but a simple modulation to B minor leads to the sudden appearance of a new theme, forte:

Ex.19

(a)

This gives place to a quiet sustained theme in B major, beginning thus:

Ex.20

It is eight bars long, and the pianoforte repeats the whole of it in richly ornamented variation—

Ex.21

&c.

expanding the close so as to lead slowly back to the tonic E: where the rondo theme again appears, with an astonishing change of tone-colour. Once more it leads to the mysterious passage quoted in No. 17. When this reaches F minor No. 19 startles us by entering in that extremely distant key. It is worked out much as on its first appearance: but no allusion is made to its

contrasted sequel, No. 20; but the rondo theme returns for the
last time in the tonic, varied as follows (cf. No. 18):

Ex.22

A solemn coda follows, developed from figure (*a*)—

Ex.23

and the movement ends quietly with an allusion to No. 17.

Like the scherzo of Beethoven's Ninth Symphony, that of the
present work is a complete first-movement in miniature, with a
first subject—

Ex.24

a second subject in the dominant, containing two themes—

Ex.25

and—

Ex.26

a development, modulating widely, combining Nos. 24 and 25,
and eventually leading to a complete recapitulation of both first
and second subjects in the tonic, with an important coda alluding
to the opening of the development, and ending with some new
triplet motion.

The trio, again, is another fully developed binary movement.
Its first subject, a canonic theme in D minor—

Ex.27

is followed by a strongly contrasted second subject in the relative major, F:

Ex.28

  This, though quite new in melody, will be seen to be identical in rhythm with the opening of the scherzo (No. 24). The development is founded entirely on this second subject, and, though short, modulates widely. The recapitulation gives No. 27 in full, making it eventually pass through the tonic major, at which point the fine effect of the bass descending chromatically bar by bar should be noted. The second subject, also in the tonic major, follows, and with a romantic variation in triplets leads towards the dominant and so to the da capo of the scherzo.

  The Finale is, on an enormous scale, that kind of rondo that most resembles a first movement with the development omitted; but here that omission is not noticeable owing to certain peculiarities in the main theme, which give its very free and expanded recapitulation much of the effect of a considerable working-out.

  The grouping of a pair of themes into a miniature binary organism is here carried out with such deliberation that after the first theme:

Ex.29

has been stated and counterstated, the second—

Ex.30

for a moment sounds like a real second subject. It leads, however, through a development of figure (*a*) (see No. 29)—

Ex.31

back to No. 29, and thence to a recapitulation of No. 30 (accompanied by (*a*) in the tonic), and a coda—

Ex.32

leads at once to the real second subject. This, again, begins with a pair of themes; the first, in E minor—

Ex.33

and the second in G major:

Ex.34

These are at once given a varied counterstatement, bringing No. 34 into E major and in canon. It is brought to a close with a new figure, which is promptly worked out at some length as a fresh canonic theme:

Ex.35

which, coming to a pause, gives place to another very broad melody, beginning in C major—

Ex.36

and closing in E. This has a full counterstatement, which ends in a cadence-subject, consisting of the new theme, No. 36 diminished in the bass, with a counterpoint above, thus:

Ex.37

This leads slowly and quietly back to the tonic A, where the first subject reappears. Brahms takes advantage of its exceptionally developed organization to produce something analogous to a working-out without the expense of a separate section, by widening the range of key and inserting some fresh thematic transformations. Thus No. 30 makes a false start in C sharp minor before finding its way to the dominant; No. 31 leads back to No. 29 in A minor, passing thence rapidly through C major to C minor, and giving rise to two developments of figure (*c*)—

Ex.38

accompanied by rhythm of (*b*) ♩ ♩ ♩ and—

Ex.39

before the recapitulation of No. 30 and the coda, No. 31, appear. These are now both in A minor. The second subject (Nos. 33 to 37) now follows in full in the tonic, without the slightest alteration. Its cadence theme (No. 37) leads quietly to the subdominant, where a new variation of the first theme (No. 29) on the lines casually suggested by No. 39, appears:

Ex.40

It is very quiet and, returning to the tonic, dies away thus—

Ex.41

giving place to an animato working up of the original figures of No. 29 (*b*) and (*c*) on a dominant pedal, which leads to a brilliant climax and the final appearance of No. 29 in a new position on the tonic, with which the Quartet ends in great triumph.

20. QUARTET IN C MINOR, OP. 60, FOR PIANOFORTE, VIOLIN, VIOLA, AND VIOLONCELLO

(1901)

Allegro non troppo. 3/4, C minor.
SCHERZO. *Allegro.* 6/8, C minor.
Andante, ¢, E major.
FINALE. *Allegro comodo,* ¢, C minor.

A FINER instance than this Quartet of the contrast between the first impressions and the facts of a new work of art could hardly be found. Although Brahms published it a little before his First Symphony, and although that symphony is in every point vastly the more difficult and complex work: in spite of an abundance of melodies of exceptional simplicity, symmetry, and breadth, such as in their very nature could not have found place in the first three movements of the First Symphony: in spite even of the advantage of remarkable terseness and extraordinary variety of style, this, the last of Brahms's Pianoforte Quartets, still remains a comparatively little-known work, for the simple and fatal reasons that it has a tragic finale, and that that tragic finale is the inevitable conclusion of the whole design

Except in times when the only criticism was popular and the only art classical, so that neither critics nor experts suffered very seriously from deceptive resemblances between true and false art, it may be doubted whether any really consistent tragedy ever met with ready contemporary approval, or was even recognized as particularly emotional. The essence of a tragedy is, surely, that while our sympathies are powerfully enlisted for the victims of the catastrophe, we are no less powerfully compelled to admire and assent to the destiny that brings the catastrophe to pass. But, unless the audience is specially trained to appreciate dramatic consistency, as must have been the case in ancient Greece and in England in the days of Queen Elizabeth, this true tragedy is never readily accepted. Contemporaries demand that if the artist is to give us a tragic conclusion at all, it must be such as to leave our sympathies wholly with the victims of the catastrophe. We have none to spare for the grandeur of the world in which they have lived—better for our pleasure that the world should be wholly bad and the catastrophe wholly unjustifiable; anything that implies the contrary is cold and academic.

Again, while fully recognizing the necessity for contrasts of mood and tone, we cannot away with anything that allows us to believe that the contrasting elements really belong to one and the same world. If we are made to feel that they do, then we either complain that they are out of touch with our sympathies, or we fail to see that they are contrasts at all, and so fall back on 'cold academicism', that catch-word of impatient and flurried judgement. The probable ground of the typical objection to the grave-diggers in *Hamlet* and the porter in *Macbeth* is that they clearly belong to the worlds in which Hamlet and Macbeth move, and jar on us accordingly, as in real life anything jars on us at the moment when it shows us that the world is larger than we bargained for. Whereas, if the porter were quite impossible in Macbeth's world and the grave-diggers quite impossible in Hamlet's, their appearance would give us no uneasy feelings: we should at once say 'Here is the necessary comic relief—now we need not trouble to follow the thread of the tragedy: thus we see what true Art is'.

The true tragedy, whether in pure music of the most 'absolute' kind or in literature, might, then, be described as a grand design, compelling our assent, and containing elements which, while making a powerful appeal to our emotional sympathies, are placed, so to speak, out of the centre of the design, so that the true and inevitable working of the design brings these emotions to a crisis as it crushes the objects of our sympathy, and leaves us, not miserable with impotent vexation, but strengthened by the conviction of its own supreme grandeur and truth. This is, of course, Aristotle's 'purging through pity and terror'; and on it depends the nobility and permanence of any artistic appeal to the emotions.

Popular and hurried criticism is apt to resent the force of the design as savouring of 'cold academicism', preferring mere misery as something far more pathetic and falling into the quaint error that there is more human sympathy in the tragedy which puts the world everlastingly in the wrong in order to bring about the useless undoing of an immaculate hero, than in the tragedy of a noble mortal whose error brings his own and others' fall in a world that would itself crash to ruin if its course were stopped to save him.

Surely there is no form of callousness so all-effacing as sentimentality? Brahms's Pianoforte Quartet in C minor has had a larger share of obloquy and misunderstanding than usually falls even to the greatest of classics. It is not my intention to prove that it is a great musical tragedy; it is absolutely impossible to prove that it, or *Hamlet*, or the *Sonata Appassionata*, or the *Agamemnon*, is a great tragedy, or that any work of art whatever is beautiful or great. If a man chooses to say that the *Sonata Appassionata* is vulgar or frivolous or ugly, there is no logical means of driving him to admit that he is wrong, so long as he gives no reasons for his statement; and then it is only his reasons which can be confuted. The position itself is impregnable from

its impertinent meaninglessness. But what can be done is to
show that certain lines and catchwords of criticism are unsound
or ambiguous and certain difficulties in the formation of opinions
very apt to be overlooked.

This short formal analysis of the Quartet will be found, as
usual, to contain little or no account of the emotional aspects of
the work. The emotions that find their place in great art are
tremendous facts, and those who talk glibly of them soon forget
and deny them.

The first subject of the first movement opens thus:

This begins again in a tone lower in B flat minor, modulates
rapidly and mysteriously, with the same figures (*a*), (*b*), and (*c*),
and ends in the following progression:

Ex.2

Here we have reached the dominant of our key (C minor).
Accordingly, it is startling to hear it turned into an E minor sixth
by the viola, pizzicato, thus:

Ex.3

This mysterious E, however, resolves upwards to F of the dominant seventh of C, and a vigorous scale—

Ex.4

firmly re-establishes our tonic, and a new development of the first theme ensues:

This leads to the transition theme—

Ex.6

which, modulating stormily to the dominant of E flat, there suddenly dies down, and after a remarkable digression to G flat and back again to E flat, slowly subsides into the second subject.

This second subject is unique in the history of musical form. It consists of a single eight-bar melody of great breadth and nobility, ending on a half-close:

Ex.7

This is followed by neither more nor less than a set of variations. The first sketches the theme in outline:

Ex.8

The second diminishes the melody of the first two bars, and brings forward a strong rhythmic figure as accompaniment:

Ex.9

This rhythmic figure runs also throughout the third variation, which is in the minor and leads, crescendo, to the fourth variation, in the major, with a close resemblance to the original theme and an effect of impassioned climax. A short cadence-subject, consisting of No. 1 in the major, with a beautiful countersubject above—

Ex.10

closes the exposition.

The development begins very quietly with No. 5, descending through treble and bass in E flat minor. Then, as the tone deepens, the semiquavers of No. 6 are added, quietly at first, till a short crescendo leads to B major (C flat) where the following new derivative of (*a*) appears fortissimo:

Ex.11

Then another form of treatment, in E minor—

Ex.12

leads to No. 11 in G major. Thereupon the second subject appears on the dominant of C minor in a form alluding to its second variation (see No. 9)—

Ex.13

and, on a dominant pedal, is worked up for more than a page in a tremendous gradual crescendo alike of tone, complexity, and passion, until the first subject reappears fortissimo, harmonized with the common chord of A flat.

Thus the recapitulation begins with none of the mystery of the opening but with the stern utterance of a fact long understood. The modulating counterstatement in B flat minor is omitted, a solemn brooding passage of simple tonality taking its place and dying into an allusion to the semiquavers of the transition theme, No. 6. Then follows the mysterious progression No. 2. The strange pizzicato E natural of the viola, No. 3, appears in its place, but surprises us now by explaining itself perfectly simply as a modulation to E minor, in which distant key the scale-figure, No. 4, quietly enters. The violin, anticipating the inevitable consequences in the near future, makes an allusion to the second subject (No. 7 (e)); the scale passage is resumed in combination with further sequences of No. 3, which moves to G major, where the whole second subject itself appears in the viola.

Such a development as this is typical alike of classical methods and of the things that make stumbling blocks for contemporary criticism. If the mysterious E natural had remained an isolated and unexplained surprise it would be far more likely to impress us on a first hearing as a stroke of genius than it possibly can now that it proves to be the greatest dramatic factor in the whole movement. It is precisely this kind of passage that we generally have in mind when we accuse Brahms of 'obscurity': the real fact of the case being that our longing for 'clearness' is singularly apt to degenerate into a desire for the gratification of our aesthetic feelings without the trouble and cost of the things which make those feelings true.

There are yet more astonishing consequences now to follow in the recapitulation, and, indeed, in the whole quartet.

The second subject is thus brought into the dominant major, a key rarely chosen for an important section of the form of a minor movement, and of altogether unique brilliance as a key for the recapitulation section, especially considering that the normal key for recapitulation is the tonic. It will be remembered that this second subject was a set of variations: which implies that its framework is exceptionally simple and recognizable. That being so, Brahms takes his advantage in the recapitulation and surprises us by three totally new variations. With any other form of second subject the result of this freedom in recapitulation would be chaos; but here, where there is, *ex hypothesi*, only one theme, and that designed for variation, an exact recapitulation would be a contradiction in terms. The surprise is, therefore, inevitable and artistic. The fourth variation returns to the old set, being on the lines of No. 9. The fifth, in continuation of the fourth, begins to modulate widely and leads, with an impassioned crescendo to (*a*) as in the development, No. 12. This becomes—

Ex.14

with extraordinarily impassioned and agitated effect, and passes
in a more sustained form—

Ex.15

back to the tonic C minor. Then, looming through volumes of
cloudy arpeggios, (*f*) from the cadence-subject (No. 10) appears,
not as at first, accompanied by (*a*). Suddenly it bursts out stormily
in a diminished form—

Ex.16

and closes into a modified version of the full cadence-subject ((*a*)
in bass and (*f*) as counterpoint), forte and in the minor; and the
movement ends slowly and solemnly but yet with startling
abruptness, since the tonic has barely yet been re-established.

This abruptness is readily explained by the short and stormy
scherzo that follows in the same key and throws comparatively
little emphasis on other keys. So long as the natural tendency
prevails to regard new sonatas as works of which the movements
are so many independent things that must stand or fall by their
equality in richness and range, so long will works in which the
movements react on each other in the profound way here exemplified be subject to misunderstanding. It is often thought specially
safe as an adverse criticism to point out that the present scherzo
is the least attractive movement in all the Pianoforte Quartets of
Brahms, but the criticism is as valueless as that which should
complain that Lear's elder daughters were among the least
attractive characters in Shakespeare.

I do not mean to draw any parallel between the characters of
this scherzo and Lear's daughters, but simply to point out that
this work is so highly organized that the movements do not stand
on their separate merits, but on their place in the whole scheme.
The terribly tragic end of the first movement has been stated
with a completeness that admits of no addition, and yet with a
suddenness that leaves us in suspense. The inevitable and
healthy reaction follows in a short movement which, *being in the*

P

same key, furnishes the tonal balance unprovided for by the end of the first movement, and, being extremely fiery and energetic, relieves our feelings by carrying us through a storm which is rather of Nature than of human passion.

The movement is fairly simple, and it will suffice merely to quote the principal figures.

1. Four introductory bars giving the initial figure of the first theme:

2. The theme itself:

3. A quiet subsidiary in the dominant:

4. The first theme diminished:

5. Several other figures rhythmically identical with (*a*), not needing quotation.

6. The impressive and mysterious middle section that fills the purpose of a trio, and is in mixed, but not remote, tonality:

This is inverted in double counterpoint—i.e. the two simultaneous themes of which it is made interchange their positions. A series of sequences on the figures of No. 18 lead with a tremendous gradual crescendo back to the first section, which is given da capo with a short coda.

The slow movement is a stream of melody that is quite easy to follow, and has probably always been recognized as one of Brahms's loveliest inspirations. Here again it will suffice to quote the beginnings of the main themes.

First, a long melody commanding attention and wonder literally from the first note, since the movement is in E major, the most distant key possible from the tonic without total loss of relationship:

Ex. 22

This eventually comes to a close, which proves to be the beginning of a transition-theme—

Ex. 23

leading to the dominant, where a pair of very light contrasted themes, forming a kind of second subject, are played with in leisurely alternation—

Ex. 24

and

Ex. 25

At last a beautiful series of drooping sequences leads slowly back through an immensely rich passage of distant keys (C major and A flat) to the tonic. At each of the two main stages of this passage the first figure of the principal theme (No. 22) appears in the bass:

Ex. 26

Thus, when the whole theme itself returns in the tonic, it appears as the third and last step in the process.

A short coda, like a miniature recapitulation of the second subject, brings forward No. 24 in the tonic, and the movement ends quietly with the first figures of the great melody with which it began.

The Finale is in full binary form, with the exposition repeated: and like all such finales is very easy to analyse. Any difficulty that may be felt in following it can only spring from its amazing emotional depth and the mystery of its development section. Its remarkable richness in devices of thematic treatment can give rise to no difficulty, for such devices can only make the form clearer. We do not follow the form through them any more than we appreciate the symmetry of a beautiful decorative design by tracing its involutions; but the complexity makes the symmetry the more forcible, for the simple reason that there are more elements to be symmetrical. What the listener must be prepared for is the profound emotional intensity and mystery of the movement, its intensely tragic end, and its force as the inevitable outcome of the previous movements.

When the first movement is as complete and far-reaching a drama as in the present work (or in the *Sonata Appassionata*, for another instance), analysis has seldom very much to say of the subsequent movements. They almost invariably express more nearly single moods than dramatic growths, and though there is an unmistakable catastrophe in the present finale, it is much more obviously foreshadowed in the spirit of the opening than it would ever be in a movement intended for the beginning of a whole work.

The first theme is a long plaintive cantabile, with a flowing accompaniment that contains a very important figure:

Ex.27

I need not quote the transition, which is in a triplet rhythm that becomes a hail-storm accompaniment to the second subject which, itself completely new in character, foreshadows in its opening notes the extraordinary developments that are soon to be made from (*a*) by augmentation:

Ex.28

This subsides into a quiet cadence-theme in equal notes—

Ex.29

which dies away in two notes—

Ex.30

which lead in the first instance to the repeat of the exposition from the outset—thus revealing themselves as the beginning of the great melody (*b*) of No. 27. In the second instance they lead on to the development, becoming—

Ex.31

(*a*) floating upwards the while. Then they become—

Ex.32

while (*a*) dies away in a chromatic scale and the violoncello introduces a new figure:

Ex.33

Then (*a*) appears augmented and doubly augmented:

Ex.34

(*a*) doubly augmented

The process is then resumed in a new sequence of keys, with the addition of the inversion of (*a*)—

Ex.35

and following otherwise much the same course as before, makes for a close in B minor, No. 33 becoming:

Ex.36

Suddenly a new version of the cadence-subject (No. 29), rich and warm in tone, enters in G major:

Ex.37

Through G minor and E flat this leads to the dominant of C minor, our tonic, where a long crescendo on (*a*) direct, inverted (see No. 35) and doubly augmented (see No. 34) leads to the first subject (*b*) in—B minor! It is accompanied by its own diminution —

Ex. 38

and, beginning softly passes crescendo to D minor, whence it proceeds in tremendous passion to the real return in C minor.

The recapitulation, beginning thus stormily, soon subsides into the quiet melancholy of its original. A simple expansion and change of harmonic trend in the sequel brings the transition and the whole second subject into the tonic, exactly reproduced.

The coda begins by carrying the cadence-subject, No. 29, in loud triumph. Herein lies the final tragic irony of the design, for this immediately brings about the catastrophe. The great first cantabile theme reappears in high rage, only to break down suddenly in an allusion to the development, Nos. 33 and 36. It is as if we now realized what lay beneath all that mystery, as broken fragments of the first theme float above and below a long tonic pedal for two wonderful pages, dying away till cut short by a final chord—in the major, but too late for happiness.

No work of art has a moral of its own; there is no answer to the questions suggested by such a tragedy as this: but all art in which emotion is ratified by design, and design vitalized by emotion, has clearly one profound moral tendency.

INDEX

'Those works to which a complete essay is devoted
have their titles printed in small capital letters.

PRINTED IN GREAT BRITAIN
AT THE UNIVERSITY PRESS, OXFORD
BY VIVIAN RIDLER
PRINTER TO THE UNIVERSITY